SAY
NO
NOW

MAKING YOU THE PRIORITY IN YOUR LIFE
NICHELE NICOLE

Book design by N.Smith

@nichele.nicole

Dedication

This book is dedicated to those who made me.

Those who supported me.

Those who loved me.

Those who used and abused me.

You all made me a better version of me…

And this ME is who SHE wants to be.

And to those that have yet to meet me…

Thank You for Supporting Me

INTRODUCTION

WHEN IS THE LAST TIME YOU SAID YES TO YOU?

For some of us, it may have been a while since we actually gave ourselves the room to be selfish and focus on us. How is this done? How do you focus on yourself? By saying NO to everyone and everything else around YOU. By redirecting your time to focus on what is most important in your life, you. By ensuring that you are making yourself a priority in your life. By Saying No Now!

This isn't a quick fix, read once, and master the skill type book. NOPE. This is a read that will make you dig deep, understand the reasons why YOU need to say NO to certain things in your life, help you acknowledge your past and instances that forced you into giving yourself away, and slowly make changes toward putting yourself first. **YES, you come first.** You come before your kids, you come before your husband, you come before your friends, you come before all else. The reason you need to say NO is that if you give all of you to everyone and everything, what do you have left for you? **Absolutely Nothing.**

We could all use some assistance in how to take our friends, family, and lovers, out of the forefront our lives for just a moment. A little help in introducing yourself to ways of making sure your focus is no longer blurred in seeking what you need to make sure your happiness is consistent. To focus solely on you will feel selfish at first, but in the end you will see and understand why saying NO is important to your success. You will be able to figure

INTRODUCTION

out why you need to Say No Now through understanding where your time and energy are being expended. You can determine the steps you can take to build on your ability to assert yourself and in the end, put the best version of you first.The hope is that at you can at least take a self reflective look at yourself and realize that you deserve more. More from yourself and more from others who've you have given yourself too. My gift is for you to learn from mistakes I've made in life, love, with family, and others. We often ask for advice to resolve our problems and rarely ever take it. Use my lessons learned and develop your own advice for yourself.

If you get nothing else but a decent read, then it's served its purpose. I sincerely hope that you learn more about yourself and determine how you WILL make yourself the priority in your life. You don't need to wait for the new year or even next week. How can you become the priority in your life today? The end goal isn't to become a narcissist, but to understand the value that YOU have. To know that your goals and dreams are in reach if you make time to make them important. To understand that you are an amazing person in yourself and no one can take that away from you. To trust that your feelings are valid and no one can tell you what your truth is. To understand that it is okay for you to say NO to anything and everything and NEVER feel guilty about it again.

THE PROCESS

UNDERSTANDING THE NEED TO SAY NO

YOURSELF

FAMILY & FRIENDS

LOVE

NOW WHAT?

UNDERSTANDING THE NEED TO SAY NO

"Those who know, do. Those that Understand, Teach." - Aristotle

UNDERSTANDING THE NEED TO SAY NO

First ask yourself, what was the last thing you said NO too? It honestly shouldn't be that difficult to come up with at least one, or even five things. You may have been shopping online and told yourself, "Nope, I don't need that new pair of shoes," or in the grocery store and said, "Not today, I'm trying to get into this dress and that Ice Cream won't help". These are common. This happens every single day. You're probably saying, "Yes, I know how to say no and do it often," this is not about you knowing how to say no, this is about you saying no to the right people and the right things at the right times. The examples given are where we say NO to ourselves. You can probably think of plenty of other times YOU denied YOU. You restricting yourself from having something you desire. You blocking yourself from a moment of happiness. You saying NO to yourself to put someone else first.

Unfortunately this is all too common for most people. We say no to ourselves only to put someone else's desires, needs, or happiness above our own. Read that again. **To put someone else's desires, needs, or happiness above YOUR OWN.** Where do you fit in? Now in some weird way, most of us will think that this makes perfect sense. That if we do more for others we will receive all of this great karma back and the blessings will be delivered tenfold upon us for all that we give. This can ring true; however the majority of the time we end up doing more for others than what we receive in return.

UNDERSTANDING THE NEED TO SAY NO

Regardless of whether the return is via the universe or your God blessing you, it often does not equal out to the energy and time you just gave up. Instead of questioning the blessings or "ju-ju" you should be receiving in return for your actions ask yourself this: Why am I willing to put my desires, needs, and happiness last? Why am I okay with saying NO to me?

I personally asked myself these questions and sadly could not give myself a quality answer for years. Much of my inability to answer this question was (or is) rooted in the roles I play in everyone else's life. I am a mother, I am a wife, I am a career driven woman, I am a daughter, I am a sister, I am a friend, and I am an advocate for others in need. I realized that I am so many things to so many people. Whenever an issue arose in any of my roles, I was there to step up and support. I put on my thinking cap, opened my heart and my ears, and sometimes loosened my purse strings, all in efforts to be what I committed to be to whomever needed me to be their "it" at that time. As I gave my all to everyone else, at the end of the day I had absolutely nothing left for me.

Not because of fatigue or lack of time, and yes those also play a part, but nothing left because I did not advocate for myself. Giving my all equated to my failing health. I was sick both mentally and physically. Stress took over my life and frustration was riding my tail.

I would snap on a moments notice then lose my shit and cry. Only to suck up my shit and say YES once again to something (or someone) I shouldn't have. Never advocating for what I needed.

As for motherhood, I embody being a mother. I work hard to prepare my child for life and I make sure she has what she needs to hopefully find success in life, but it's a selfless job. You give everything you have and often times the little you don't have to give and usually get nothing in return. I am also a wife. This is also a selfless job. You are the friend, confidant, therapist, fixer, cook, and cleaner (at times) for a person you have committed your life too. Marriage is a shared commitment. There are days where one party may feel like they've given all they can. Days where the other pushes thought fatigue, hurt, or pain to make sure your love for the other party is visible. Those times where someone is expected to come before you.

Most reading this will say, well you signed up for all of this shit and now you're complaining about it. Why? I'm not complaining, I'm just telling my truth. Often times we don't sign up for it and even when you do, you couldn't have predicted the outcome if you want4ed to. Through life, we will unknowingly walk into some roles and accept the responsibility that comes with it. The commitment of most roles, just like a job, often changes as time goes on.

UNDERSTANDING THE NEED TO SAY NO

For instance, what I was responsible for as a mother of a toddler is not the same as the responsibilities of a mother of a teenager. I am still committed to being a mother, but it's different.

As a friend, your friendship may start off as a social connection and through the trials and tribulations of life, you become a confidant, a therapist, an ATM, a hype man, a matchmaker and everything else for your friends. As a wife, the role changes as the years pass. You give a little and you gain a little, but through the trials and tribulations of marriage you lose a little bit of yourself as well. It's not a bad thing, but it's a real thing. When two become one, that it gets real. Compromise is beautiful; however as a spouse you may at times find yourself compromising at the cost of you. Saying YES to things you don't desire to do, things that do not interest you. You find yourself losing the ability to say NO at times.

So did you sign up for it? Did you assume all of this would come with any of these roles when you made these choices in life? Absolutely Not! You take it in stride and do what you have to do. You said YES to all of it and never stopped to question anything. Or maybe you did question it, but pushed past your doubt, because that's what being a great mom, friend, lover, or spouse is supposed to do, right? The key takeaway is that you have pushed yourself into the role of saying YES.

UNDERSTANDING THE NEED TO SAY NO

Not yes to everything your kids, spouse, lover, friends, or job wants. You say YES to putting them above you. YES to making the needs of all of these titles, areas, and categories above the needs of yourself. In the end you haven't said NO to anyone but YOU.

Saying NO is necessary. Why? Because when you Don't Say No...

Others Priorities become more important than YOURS

Strangers take time from YOU, Family, and Your friends

You lose the ability to replenish yourself

You become frustrated and stress among others happiness

You are unable to say YES to the important things (YOU)!

Think these reasons sound selfish? Then this may not be the read for you. Continue giving yourself away to everyone. Continue saying YES to everything and anything. Continue giving more of you than what you have to offer. Continue to say NO to YOU. Continue to put yourself on the back burner and make everyone else more important than you. **Continue to say NO to the most important person in your life, YOU!**

Rules and boundaries were pivotal in me making a major change for me. The areas (or things) that I decided to say NO too are bolded throughout this book. Again, these are my rules and boundaries.

Hopefully they provide you with some perspective and help you start your own process of asserting yourself and taking back your time. While reading you should ask yourself "Do these rule and boundaries apply to the changes I want to make?" and "Am I ready to say NO and start saying YES to me?". The last question is one that you can answer to yourself. The only thing needed is an open mind and an open attitude ready for change.

NO, I WILL NOT PUT MY WELL BEING ON THE BACK BURNER

Your personal well-being matters. If you do not put a focus on you, then who will? It's easy to assume that your friends, family, your spouse, your lover, your kids, will be the ones to pick up the pieces until it comes time for action. During the times in which we need someone the most, many times no one shows up or we do not speak up. Think about what you will change if you start to say NO. You can focus on the possible negative outcomes like, "So and so will be mad at me" or "They will think I don't care" and "I will come off as selfish". All of these are TRUE! And who gives a damn.

You have allowed others to manipulate your decisions and responses for long enough. It's now time to make a decision that will set you up for long term success. It is now time for you to say NO to others and other things in your life and start saying YES.

Saying YES to YOU! The only things you have to lose by saying no are individuals and distractions who were not positively adding to your life. I repeat, by saying NO - **THE ONLY THING YOU LOSE IS THE BULLSH*T IN YOUR LIFE!**

But what you gain is bigger than anything you lose. You gain more energy. You gain more time. You will improve your confidence (it is scary to say no at first, but you will get the hang of it). You take back the control you lost - control of your decisions and control of how you live your life. You gain the respect of others. You have more fun! Where is the downside?

So how do you put a NO into action? The reason the action is important is that often times telling someone to do something is 1000% easier than them actually following through with it. Saying no is one of the hardest actions many people face on a daily basis. To ease into it you first need to understand why the need exists for you to start saying no.

NO, I WILL MAKE A CHANGE

Something transpired in your life for you to make the determination that you need to improve on being able to say NO to either yourself or others. That you need to assert the importance of YOU over others. Whatever that dilemma or issue was, does not really matter.

UNDERSTANDING THE NEED TO SAY NO

All that matters is that you recognized there was a problem. Pat yourself on the back for that! This is the hardest part; being honest with yourself and choosing to improve. But this is only the first step. Just because we see a problem in our lives, many of us choose to run and look the other way.

We ask ourselves if the issue is really disrupting our every day lives. We question how great the impact is to all of the other things we like to do. We then make excuses, yes excuses, for why its "not really that big of an issue" then we go on with the same shit only to complain over and over again. The issue may not even be your own. This same mess resinates with our family and friends. We will make excuses for why their issues, that impact our lives, are not really major issues for us at all. We will make excuses for why the unnecessary things that take time away from what is important to us aren't really "that bad" in the overall scheme of our lives. Oh My God - this gets so old.

Stop with the excuses and just say NO. Say Nah. Say Nope. I don't care how you choose to say it, just say it and understand that you giving all of YOU away to the unnecessary is not a way of life. You deserve better. So take the first step in understanding that you have an area of your life where you need to say NO. This is just the tip of the iceberg. As they say, to move forward you must know and understand from which you came. So let's acknowledge some of the mistakes so we can move on.

<u>NO, I WILL ACKNOWLEDGE MY WRONGS AND BE ACCOUNTABLE</u>

Now that you know why you need to Say NO, there is additional work to be done in acknowledging how we got here. Oh yeah - much of this lies with you and not others or things. You allowed yourself to get to a point of saying YES to everything and everyone. You permitted people and things to take away your time from YOU. You made space for anything to be more important than YOU. Now we have to come with terms with why.

For me, much of the reason why I became reluctant to say No was rooted in my need for acceptance. I grew up with an older sibling who was 10+ years older than me (talk about a shadow for your ass). She had the world at her fingertips and stars in her sights. She was going to be famous. For her, my parents made ways out of no ways and much of the focus was on her. All of my family and friends assumed the best and also focused on her rise to success. My sister was also the queen of telling people what she was doing for herself and what she wasn't going to do for others. I came to understand that she minimized the expectations of reciprocity from her and increased her expectation of support.

Her time was focused on her to be successful and you either rode with her or got off the train. I saw the good and bad of this. Some people hated her, hated on her, and more wanted to be in her presence.

UNDERSTANDING THE NEED TO SAY NO

I wanted people to want me as much as they desired to be around my sister, so I become the fixer. I became the helpful one. I became the one that never said NO. It was a beginning to an end for me.

Long story short, my sister chose her path in entertainment and still has her sights set on notoriety, but regardless of where she is in her career she still stands firm in her protection of self and her time. I ended up being the YES girl through life, love, and career. In the end, I had to acknowledge that all of the people I had chosen to say yes too were only partly at fault. The majority of the fault rested with me. Allowing myself to focus on what I didn't have versus focusing on what I desired thrust me into a world of giving myself, my time, and my focus to others and leaving nothing for me.

When you are taking account of why you are reluctant to Say No, you must first hold yourself accountable by acknowledging your past - both good and bad, as many times there was an event (or events) that brought about our current actions, whether good or bad. Acknowledgement can be difficult. It is easier to make excuses or place full blame on another party instead of owning the cause for our behavior. You must Say NO to this. This is the first step to taking ownership of you. Own your Shit!

Once you can acknowledge the reason why you are hesitant to Say NO, only then can you move forward with reclaiming your time, refocusing on your goals, and making YOU a priority with the ability to effectively prioritize others in your life.

NO, YOU WILL HONOR MY RULES AND BOUNDARIES

In every area of life, there are rules and there are boundaries. Where we decided to break the rules or push the boundaries is based on how risk adverse we are. Are you up for the challenge to break your own rules by saying NO? If not, go back and reassess your understanding and re-acknowledge the need to say no in your life. To fully embrace the need to Say NO, you will need to establish rules and boundaries. This is not only for you, but mostly for others. Your largest task will be the enforcement of these rules and standing strong in your boundaries. Here are some of the rules I set for myself to ensure I could stand strong in my NO.

My Priorities Come First!

Set your priorities in order of importance. My priorities are Personal Time, Personal Goals, Family, Career, and Friends. They matter to me in this order and will often times intersect with one another.

However; no one can come and place their priorities in my life. No one is allowed to rearrange my priorities to work for their lives. If I am not allowed to make sure that I'm good first, then I am unable to truly focus on anything else.

My Priorities Matter

It is a hard NO for me to engage in a conversation to defend my priorities. I will change the order of importance when I feel it is needed. You need to establish a similar rule. No one can make you feel any guilt for putting the importance of a priority over something else in your life. Most of us let this happen regularly, especially moms and wives. How in the hell is someone going to tell you why your nail appointment should be less important than you kids or husband? Do they know how well your home is cared for? Have they seen or heard otherwise that would give them permission to pass judgement? NO! By letting someone else dictate your priorities you have once again said YES and that stops right here, right now.

I Have the RIGHT to be Selfish

Your selfishness is healthy. It is okay to be selfish and love yourself without ignoring the needs of others.

UNDERSTANDING THE NEED TO SAY NO

You will learn more about navigating through the statement of "You're Selfish" that will be received as you begin to Say No to the requests of others, not their needs. You can always support YOU first while assisting others, but remembering that it is key to keep you first.

Negativity will No Longer be Accepted

This does not to mean that others will not be negative towards your change. Change is difficult and there are so many of us who do not know how to deal with change. Oh well, it is not your job to convince others that your change is beneficial for them. The changes you make (or are making) are for YOU! I refuse to tolerate negativity. This includes doubt, this includes the naysayers, this also includes those who are negative about their own possibilities. I say NO from the door. The reason being is that energy transfers. We all know that misery loves company and this is no different. If a situation feels negative, I say NOPE, and maneuver on. It comes off as selfish, it comes off as arrogant in certain situations, but it protects me from bad energy and drama.

As I said, these are some of my personal rules and trust, others create themselves as I navigate my life. For me, rules equal boundaries. I say NO to allowing others to push these boundaries. YES, people will try you and test you.

UNDERSTANDING THE NEED TO SAY NO

What you have allowed in the past is for people to trample on your boundaries and contain your actions within their boundaries. It works for them. You had no rules for yourself, but were restricted to what others wanted for you. No more. Starting today you are making a change to say NO. You are saying that YOU require, not deserve, but require respect in regard to your life, your priorities, and whatever else you deem as important.

<u>NO MORE PROCRASTINATION - ONLY ACTION</u>

Those who are most successful in life are selfish. No, it is not because they have money to be selfish. No, it is not because they have a large staff to delegate their responsibilities too. It is because they have put themselves first to ensure they can be available, when needed, for others. Most successful people take the beginning and end of their day for themselves. Why? Because they know they are important to themselves.

I am not talking monetary success. Success is subjective, but I am talking about success in terms of your internal peace and happiness. If you have neither, how do you focus on anything else. Put your decision into action and Say NO. Through setting boundaries, you will establish the order of importance in your life. Some of these areas will most likely go hand in hand with one another. So let's get started.

UNDERSTANDING THE NEED TO SAY NO

For me, my priorities revolved around Time, Personal Goals, Family, Career, and Friends. I had to Say NO to requests and things that impacted these areas, in this order, to make more time for me to be successful in my personal life. I read self-help books, watched Ted Talks, spoke to others in my organization who had obtained the success I sought, and even with all of this, I still didn't get it. I felt like I was doing all of the things right, I was working long hours (12+ hours a day), I was making great money ($80K+ a year), my family appeared happy, I had a great title, and my friends were there if I needed them. What the hell was the issue? **The issue was me.** I put action behind things others told me too, but nothing behind what I needed. I had to Say NO.

What did I Say NO to? I said NO to the abuse of my time. What does this mean? This meant that me working 12+ hours a day only to then come home and continue working was not logical. It impacted other areas as well. My personal goals were never going to be achieved because I did not make time for me. That was a major NO. Time given to my job was taken away from my family and my goals, but the little time that I did have and would have liked to spend to myself, I would give to my family too. My husband and child still needed me. My friends, well what are those? I hadn't met up or seen anyone (unless you count Facebook and Instagram) in ages. I was a ghost friend. This was all because I allowed someone else to control my time.

UNDERSTANDING THE NEED TO SAY NO

Where the abuse of my time benefit me was in my career. Again, I was the YES girl, the hard worker, the fixer. My inability to Say NO to everything else, made me shine in the area that I thought defined success. It didn't. I watched others around me advocate for themselves and become abused by the organization I had worked so hard for. You became a leper if you stood your ground and took ownership of your life. A personal life was non-existent and that was the expectation. My action was a career change, an immediate career change. My goals and hard work have not yet allowed me to work 100% for myself, I found an organization that values time and balance. While I am still a real person, with real bills who needs to work, I am also a human being who needs rest and time to process my thoughts. In choosing me, I gave up money, but gained clarity in understand that slaving for take-home pay was not worth the loss of my time. I was working extremely hard for money that I couldn't enjoy. In the end, it was an easy NO that came hard at first.

Now it is your turn to be assertive. Not just for something to do, but to change your current way of life. To further free up your time, your space, your heart from the burdens placed on them by others. **NOW IS YOUR TIME TO SAY NO!**

YOURSELF

When you know yourself, No one else's opinion matters

Unknown

<u>YOU IS SMART. YOU IS KIND. YOU IS IMPORTANT.</u>

This line always causes me to bust out in laughter. If you've seen the movie *The Help*, you know that a woman struggling to keep herself and family afloat is seen sowing positivity into a child that she works for. She tells the child to value herself and her importance in the world, but it took the whole film and a bad ass friend for her to realize how much she mattered to herself and those around her.

If you ask most people, "Who is the most important person in your life?", the answer is often someone else besides themselves. A key family member, a spouse, a child (or children), a pet, but rarely is it themselves. In society, to state that you are most important to you is viewed as narcissistic. To say that you care about your personal well-being over that of others is selfish. To regard yourself and the time that you need over someone's desires of you is met with criticism. Why? Because society has convinced us that being a "good person" is doing for others on a continuous basis. That putting yourself last somehow constitutes a level of perfection.

Selfish behavior is often described as immoral. A good person thinks of others first. By you choosing you, you are paying too much attention to your own wants, needs, and well-being, and not enough attention to others.

So how dare you put yourself first, right? WRONG! If you truly believe that your own personal happiness and well being are rooted in you caring and doing for others, then have at it. But ask yourself one question: What happens when you have nothing more to give?

What happens when you get sick? What happens when you physically don't have yourself to give? You can live in the "I Think" and "Shoulda, Coulda, Woulda's" all day, but you couldn't bet money on who would pick up all of the crumbling pieces for you if they fell in the midst of you providing for everyone. No one is going to take care of everything for you.

NO ONE WILL CARE ABOUT YOU MORE THAN YOU

It's that simple. Not your spouse. Not your lover. Not your kids. For damn sure, not anyone at work. Not your clients. Not your family. No one but YOU can put you first. Let that sink in. Mentally dispute it if you need too and come up with the list of names that you "know" would come to your rescue and you "know" care about you more than they care about themselves. If you do have a list of individuals that care about (or for) you more than themselves, then hand them a copy of this book too, lol. Why does someone else care more about your well-being than you do for yourself?

YOURSELF

While it sounds great, it is not healthy and it's not sustainable. The others in your life have priorities too. So, at the moment when they are needed and are not available, it is only you that is there for YOU.

NO, I AM MY MOST VALUABLE ASSET

It can be hard to verbally speak about our value to ourselves and we will instead put time and effort into everyone and everything else to make up for what we don't find within. This has sadly been the case for me. Ask anyone about me and you'll get the same answers: She's Reliable. She's Hardworking. She's So Sweet. She's So Helpful. She's So Trustworthy. All of these responses are rooted in all of the things that I have done for others. What you will not hear is someone saying, "Gosh she takes good care of herself." NEVER. Because I didn't. Taking care of me was foreign to me.

My internal response was always, "I'll be okay" or "I'm fine" or in layman's terms, "NO Self. You are not worthy of the time you deserve." As you work through the reasons and who you say YES too, I want you to further understand the need to say NO. Let's start by saying NO to yourself. Now, you're probably thinking, "Why would I say NO to myself"...well in all honesty you're not.

YOURSELF

You are saying NO to all of the shit and people you would have said YES too. You're saying NO to allowing yourself to be taken advantage of by anything and everything that is not benefitting you. You're saying NO to putting yourself last. **From this point forward, You Come First.**

❖ No, you will no longer allow self doubt to discourage you.

❖ No, you cannot take time away from yourself for someone else.

❖ No, you will no longer postpone your goals and dreams.

❖ No, I am not going to make myself last in my life.

You are the most important thing in your life. Your needs, your desires, your wants, they all matter. No, they don't have to matter to others, your opinion of you is all that matters. Stop placing your importance in the hands of others. Your goals and dreams will never come to fruition if you constantly wait for someone else to validate their importance. It will not happen. NO, your goals and dreams are not important to others - they are important to YOU! They matter the most to YOU. You are the reason they will come to fruition, not others.

NO, I WILL NO LONGER BE EMOTIONALLY EXPLOITED

Another big reason that you we say NO to ourselves is emotional exploitation. This is where someone in your life exploits your emotions and the action they cause you to take for their personal gain. For many of us, this occurs with our family and friends, and we will dig deeper into this topic later in the book. For many of us, this is what has probably been going on in your life for quite some time now. The most common scenario: Someone has an issue. They come to you in a heightened emotional state. They don't know how they can resolve the issue without you. Sound familiar?

This is where your YES steps in to save the day. You feel emotionally inclined to help. You don't want to see someone you care about in a bind, hurting, or in need. Your emotions overshadow your ability to see the whole picture and take into consideration all aspects of the situation. You don't stop to ask the why, how , when, or where questions to discern what's really going on. If you ask too many questions, now you seem like an asshole. What you do see is fear, you see desperation, you see a way for you to be the savior. [Insert your superhero theme song here] So, you do what you do best and you step in to save the day.

Whether your version of "saving" someone is offering advice to aide them through a resolution or physically offering yourself up to resolve the issue, you have made a way out of no way and now they feel better. They feel safe. Their emotional stress has been removed. But where did the stress go?

YOURSELF

It doesn't just disappear. NO, it's been transferred to you. Your emotions have now been exploited. Now you feel worry, concern, or anger (depending on the situation) for this persons issues.

This issue is now taking up precious space in your mind as you contemplate if you did enough, do they need more advice or help, what happens now after they leave you. You have again said NO to yourself and used your time to give others more of YOU. This is a one-sided transaction. This type of selfishness is where someone gets what they need from you without putting anything back into you. Now think about how many times and how many people this scenario (or a similar one) has been repeated in your life. Can you even calculate how much time that it took for you to help resolve any and every issue brought your way? How many of these same people were a trusted resource for your issues? For most of us, the number of people will not be the same. For me, the one-sided relationships I allowed in my life was astonishing.

Our time and energy are part of our emotional accounts. Too many withdrawals and you end up with a negative balance and you don't have any energy left for you. This is the type of selfishness you need to avoid like the plague. This selfishness doesn't just come from those we know, this also comes from many we don't. The calls and requests for donations. Many for a good cause, but its emotional exploitation.

YOURSELF

These tug at your heart, make you feel as though you have it going way too good, make you feel the detriment of others and feel guilty for your way of life. Your guilt becomes compelling and it compels you to give, either physically or monetarily.

Now how much of an ass would I be for saying don't give when a charitable request comes your way, a big one right? NO. The goal is not to become a scrooge type individual in terms of giving. You should give where you feel compelled to do so. You should help, you should give your time (or money where able) back to your community and other causes that you feel connected to. You should feel comfortable in Sayin NO to those you don't. The goal is to stop saying YES to every fucking thing that tugs at your emotions. Say NO to the lies. Say NO to the time suckers. Say NO to the stuff that takes away the precious time you need for you. Become selfish and say YES to your needs.

Society has convinced us that being selfish is bad, but bad for who? Others? Well, yeah, because they are put last. Not placed last because of some societal bias, but placed last in terms of where they rank in the hierarchy of your personal life. This is OKAY. What's not okay, is where people use their selfishness to emotionally exploit you. Key indicators of manipulation are manipulation of facts (aka Lies), overwhelming you with data (facts and statistics) to prove you wrong, little or no time to decide, and constant judging or criticism. All of these are ways others exploit us, but again the focus is not on changing them but to change YOU. You are often your times worst enemy.

You Treat Yourself Worse than Everyone Else

Catch this. You will exploit yourself worse than anyone every could. You say, "No one exploits me?" but these are Lies. I don't care how attractive, amazing, smart, intelligent, street smart, or whatever other fancy adjective you want to use to label yourself, we have all been manipulated at some point and time. To be honest, the biggest exploiter of you is YOU. Let's take these key indicators one by one to break down how we emotionally manipulate ourselves.

Manipulation of Facts: Have you ever lied to yourself? Told yourself that a situation was not as bad as it appeared to be? Made excuses for others behaviors towards you. Justified your actions even though you know you were wrong. YES, we all have. Most of us do it on a daily basis. Say NO to this detrimental behavior. This is part of your acknowledgement of the need to change. If something seems bad, it probably is. For me, the areas where I manipulated the facts were often in my career, in my finances, and in love. I would tell myself that I was doing better than others to boost myself up. Instead, I should have said NO girl! You are not doing as well as YOU COULD be doing.

YOURSELF

In my finances, I would lie to myself instead of believing the facts that my bank account said "You Ain't Got It" or "you don't need any new anything" and "if they can afford it, so can I" only forcing myself into additional debt or feeling upset with myself after making bad financial decisions. Lastly, oh love. It goes without saying because I cannot count how many times I convinced myself that someone loved me or cared about me because it is what I wanted. I had to come to terms that this had to stop for me.

Facts are facts. Many of our current situations are not where we want them to be and you know what needs to happen to get where you want to be. So to get from Point A to Point Z, the finish line, stop mentally manipulating your situation. Stop telling your friends, family, and others who truly do not care lies that make things seem better. Stop posting a glimpse of what you think success looks like and take the time to do the work to have the success you seek. Make Your Change Today. Tell yourself NO to faking it and put action behind what you've been saying you are "going to" do. No more saying what you are GOING to do and more of what you WILL do.

Sounds simple, right? Sadly it isn't and change takes time. Many of us have been trained to lie to ourselves our entire lives. Lies often feel better than the truth.

YOURSELF

We've been trained to convince ourselves that life should be a bed of roses at all times. It's not and won't be if you do not stop lying to yourself first, your lies force you to have a hard time making change in other areas of your life and with other people. Accept your current reality and accept where change is needed.

Say NO to your past actions and Make Change. Say NO to mediocrity in EVERY area of your life. Do the work. Start that business. Write that book. Go back to school. Apply for that job. Save that money. Take that trip. Move to a new city. Whatever it is, say NO to lying about when it will happen and make it happen. When you change your "I'm Gonna" to an "I Will" you will the power of controlling your outcome so you will be successful. You WILL win this year, next year, and for years to come. You WILL no longer have to live a lie because you are building the truth.

Another big one for me was constant criticism or judgement. We can all pin point one person who is skilled at making us feel like trash with their words. Most of the time it is a family member or old friend (we will discuss these individuals later). For me it was (and still is at times) me. I was (and still am) my biggest critic. If anyone knows how make me feel down and ignore any and all accomplishments of mine, it's me! The biggest area I criticized myself in was my worth and my value. Not just in love, but in life. I had the drive and the ability to do so much, but never felt that I was worth the risk or the reward.

YOURSELF

This kind of thinking is manipulating and can have long term, irreparable impacts. When young people are unable to validate their worth and personal value, they become grown people who seek validation from others.

If you Say NO to only one thing, say NO to allowing yourself to be manipulated. Say NO to the doubt within. Most importantly, say no to your internal voice in you that says you are not qualified for that promotion. The voice that tells you that you are a bad mom because you missed something at your kids school. The feeling that makes you think you are inadequate as a spouse because your partner isn't happy at the moment. It sounds like doubt when you are trying to make change in any area of your life.

You Control Your Ability to be Accountable: The biggest thing you will gain from Saying NO to yourself, is control. Again, the ability to have control over your emotions, your decisions, and how you choose to use yourself. You no longer grant anyone or anything the ability to make their truth about your reality. Your doubt will no longer control your every move. You will control YOU. To start, take an accounting of your life. Are you where you want to be?

This does not have to apply to every area of your life, but it matters if it only represents one area. If you are not where you want to be, ask yourself why?

YOURSELF

This is not the question to blame everyone else in your life for why you didn't "make it". This is to truly understand what sections of your life are currently incomplete by your own standards. Where do you need to put in the work to complete the task? Let's take my education for a scenario:

I met my husband and at the time only had a few college classes under my belt. I had a steady job and made great money. My job didn't require me to have any additional skills or education so I had not a care in the world. My husband and I discussed moving to a new state for new opportunities. In efforts to move, I needed to find a job. As I began to look for jobs I realized that the requirements were not the same from state to state. Many of the positions that paid a decent wage required a degree. For many years, I had put it on the back-burner. It was a goal of mine, but it wasn't important. My parents weren't riding my ass about it and my life was decent. I had all of the things that I felt I deserved. Until I realized I didn't. I didn't have the luxury of flexibility. I couldn't pick up and move, not for lack of skills, but for lack of effort. My choice not to put forth the effort to complete my college degree limited my ability and the ability of my family from having options. So what now?

Some of you are probably saying, well he (my husband) should have been understanding and I should have kept my good job, right? No, because it wasn't about him. **Again, the reason why I hadn't chosen to go back to college had nothing to do with my husband. I had constantly told myself I didn't need it.** I told myself I needed to wait until my child got older to go back to school. I convinced myself that my career was good enough and a degree wouldn't make that much of a difference. I said NO o the value of education in my life.

Then I said, Nah! I had to take accountability and acknowledge that I had set myself back in so many ways. I had emotionally exploited myself with lies to manipulate my truth. I had to put in the work to make myself complete. 2015 - Bachelors and then 2017 - Masters and honestly it was easier than I assumed it would be because I changed my thinking. I told myself that I needed it. It was no longer an option, I needed to improve myself like now! I said NO to only having a limited availability of job opportunities. I said NO to having my earning potential capped. I said NO to limiting my ability (and that of my family) to be flexible in where we lived and/or worked. My change had nothing to do with anyone else and everything to do with me.

A change like this or my scenarios doesn't just apply to education. This applies to any and everything. I have spoken to so many people with so many amazing ideas, but because they say YES to doubt, they don't may any moves.

YOURSELF

When we speak again, it's the same wish for an opportunity, the same eagerness for change, the same voice of doubt that keeps them in the same place they started. NO, NO, NO!

NO, I NEED AND DESERVE TIME TO MAKE A CHANGE

I want more for YOU. I want you to want more for yourself in every area of your life. In the next 30 days take the time to make your goals and aspirations a priority. You may not accomplish a single goal in the next month, but you can make some headway towards the finish line if you want to. For the next 30 days, Say NO to everything that is a distraction from your goals. Let's call it a Focal Fast. You are going to try to abstain from people and things that take you off of your path. Pick one goal, just one to start and make it a focal point.

Make the time and stick to it. Successful leaders block out time in their calendars for every minute of their day, including themselves and you should be no different. We use our phones to track every move in everyone else's lives, so use it to benefit yours. Calendar at least 30 minutes every day to focus on you. 30 minutes out of a 24 hour day is not much at all. The average person spends 2.5 hours on social media per day. What's 30 minutes less redirected on you? You want to start a business, research the requirements to start the business in your city and state. Do you have the money   needed to launch your business, NO? Well research how to get a loan...Don't have the credit score for a loan - NO? Start with what you got in your bank account. But you don't have the resources, Right? WRONG. We have the resources for Whatever We Want to have the resources for! They may not be tangible but you have the access and the ability to make change so you can access them. If it's money, redirect some of your funds to your business savings. Again, focusing on the small changes needed for making you a priority.

You will be amazed by the outcome even if its only clarity for your life. Clarity in determining the path needed to accomplish your goals. Clarity in understanding who is for you and who isn't. You can even use the time to work on you, try a new workout class. Get a massage, Do Yoga, or Meditate. This isn't the time when you go get your hair and/or nails done. This is the time when you are alone with YOU. From personal experience, this can be scary to be with your own thoughts and truly hear your voice. Your voice might have been silent for so long that you need to rediscover it, so take this time to do just that.

Whatever it takes, the answer is NO to everything else and YES to focusing on what will add value to your life, what will stop you from manipulating the truth, and allow you to say YES to YOU!

FRIENDS & FAMILY

"Anything is possible when you have the _right_ people to support you"

Misty Copeland

FRIENDS & FAMILY

This topic is an area that many of us struggle. We are taught that the family is the backbone of our lives. Without your family you are nothing. Family is everything. Blood is thicker than water. Need I go on...NO. This topic is a struggle because we along with generations prior to us have been emotionally manipulated to believe that family can disrespect, disappoint, and demean you and it all be okay because...They're Family!

Second to ourselves, our family has a brilliant way of emotionally exploiting us in every way. Forcing us into situations in which we provide a level of forgiveness that we wouldn't give our worse enemy. Accepting treatment that you wouldn't consider dishing out on your worse day. Causing us to make time for drama and other unnecessary moments that no one would ask to participate in. And again, because it's your family. Through your personal growth and your journey, you will realize that there are family members who we need to love from afar. Not because you do not love them, but in order to keep loving them, distance is a requirement. Think about these individuals who you love from afar - what placed them in this position? How egregious were their actions that forced you to cut them off? Lastly, do their actions mimic the actions of other family members who are closer to you?

Let's not forget friends. These are the individuals that we choose to bring into our lives who usually become family.

FRIENDS & FAMILY

These individuals are special because to really be considered a friend, this person has had your back when your family was ghost. These people held you accountable on your actions when you tried to manipulate the situation. These people are the real MVP's in your life on most days. Yet, friends have their own special category that we need to put them in to Say NO. These individuals take a close third to family in the hierarchy of emotional exploitation. We take on titles with their kids (God Parents, Aunt, Uncle, etc.), we work to make a way for them at times when no way exists, as you may have operated as an ATM (probably more than once) for "that" friend when times got rough. These people also know you at your worse.

I personally feel that many people use the term friend way too loosely. Everyone is a friend but many do nothing to deserve the title or keep it in tact. If I think back over the past 20 years of my life, I've had plenty of best friends, I'd say at least 4. To date, I have 3 real friends. Two are not the same people from 20 years ago. Why? I held myself accountable for the drama that occurred in our relationship, the manipulation I allowed, and I decided to move forward with my life without them in it. This was part of my personal growth. We all have heard that everyone has a season in your life and damn if that isn't true. We change, your change may have you looking similar on the outside, but you have changed. Sort of like a tree.

FRIENDS & FAMILY

The tree that shed its leaves 20 years is not the same tree we see today. It has gone through so many seasons that included beautiful sunny days and weathering many storms, but through it all the tree evolved. Damn it, I'm a tree. You are a tree, we are all trees and we evolve and as you evolve, either your friends and circle evolve too or you build a new circle. Simple as that. Everyone doesn't get a front seat and you don't have to tote their baggage on your journey. You only impact your growth when you limit your growth because of your friends or your family. You hurt yourself emotionally when you make excuses for any ignorance from family. So, no different from any other area, you need rules and boundaries because we have to sometimes Say NO to our friends and family too.

NO, MY FAMILY DOES NOT GET A PASS TO DISRESPECT ME

One thing that kicked off my ability to Say NO to a lot of areas in my life was recognizing that disrespect from family is still disrespect. Even when its from your own immediate family. Now everyone's family has made comments and ragged on their life choices because in reality we've probably made some messed up decisions at one point or another. What is not okay is when commentary transforms into blatant disrespect. Disrespect to the point that your feelings are no longer up for consideration.

FRIENDS & FAMILY

Families have a way of telling you what will and won't come to fruition through their personal knowledge and what they love to call "experience". Everyone has been through something and will tell you why your dreams are just smoke. Our closest relatives love to root their commentary in #Facts or "The Truth" because if they don't give it to us then who will. No one. The reason is because half of what they say is ignorance and it's disrespectful.

I have received commentary about my weight, my appearance, my choice in who I am dating, how I choose to date, where I work, how I spend my money, how I raise my child, my choice of husband, and basically every subject under the sun. Simply put, it's disrespectful. We would never even fix our mouth to comment or tell someone to adjust their way of life especially if there was no request to do so. So why do we let our family do it? Go ahead and say it, because they are family. Its okay because its your mom, your dad, your sister, your aunt. NO, it's not. Disrespect in any form is never okay and it doesn't mater who the person is. Disrespect is sometimes dished out like this:

Disgrace - Someone in your family (or our friends) pokes fun at or insults another friend or family member Name calling, body shaming, attacking someone's way of life or their character, it is all in efforts to disgrace someone. We have all been to that family function or with our friends and the commentary always funny when its not you.

FRIENDS & FAMILY

We all dive in on the family member screw up of the year - but remember even though it may not be your turn now, it may come soon.

Drama Filled Adjectives - Those closest to us can use indirect methods to hurt us as well. Family and friends who have some type of feeling towards your choices love to add key words like "always" "never" "all" "none" oh and one of my favorites is "little". These words are used to dramatize the conversation to shame you into being passive in our receipt of the disrespect. Like "You always dating someone new" or "I see you got your little business up and running". We chuckle or walk away in shame and sometimes never hear it because its behind our backs, but these words are used to minimize or shame you about your way of life.

Dictating - Our parents (and other elders) are good at this and don't seem to know when to move on and let you Do YOU. This is where our family members feel they can give orders on our life. Someone telling you that, "You need to support your sister" or "You got money so you can help" are some examples in how our families love to dictate how we maneuver in the world through disrespecting our opinion or ability to have self control.

All of these forms of disrespect are harmful in so many ways. Words mean something and words can hurt.

For many of us disrespect is a repetitive norm that we have grown up witnessing and wouldn't know where to begin to create change. Well, the change always starts with YOU. Speak Up and Stand Up in that you will no longer tolerate anyone's disrespect in your life. Family or not. As someone who understands their value and acknowledges where you need to change, understand that any disrespect dished needs to halt as well. We cannot ask for change in others, especially our family, and not be willing to change ourselves.

NO, OUR (BLOOD) BOND DOESN'T FORGIVE YOUR FUCKERY

What is fuckery? Fuckery is where our family members love to show their natural ass (in public or private) and then expect you to overlook the aftermath. You might have a sibling who gets themselves into sticky situations. Your mothers way of expressing her thoughts come out in very unnecessary actions. Your cousin might be on some bullshit in living off of your elders but that's not your business. Nah. This is fuckery and we are experts in looking past fuckery, giving passes for fuckery, and talking to everyone else but the person creating the fuckery about the fuckery. It has to stop.

Let me give you an example of the fuckery I had to Say NO too:

My Story: Thanksgiving Fuckery

During a recent Thanksgiving, my husband and I had a disagreement. We were in the private confines of our master bedroom with the door closed. My mother was visiting from out of town and was in the adjacent living room during this disagreement. The disagreement escalated into an argument. We began to raise our voices. My husband stood up to leave the room to give us some space and I, in my frustrated state, grabbed his hand to stop him from walking out of our bedroom. He shouted "You better get your fucking hands off of me." Just then our bedroom door burst open, there was my mother angry and enraged. She hollered at my husband, "Don't you fucking put your hands on her!".

I stood there shocked. What ever gave my mother the impression that my husband put his hands on me. I hadn't hollered out. I wasn't screaming - hell, we weren't screaming. What drama had she assumed was occurring behind our bedroom door that made her react like that? My husband responded that he didn't touch me, but my mom was fired up and ready for a fight. A fight with my husband. Before I could get a word out or before my husband could explain, she let into him in what she thought was my protection. My mom called him every thing and I just recall being witness to the unfolding of my family in front of my face.

FRIENDS & FAMILY

My child came to assist and tried her best to calm my mother down, but it did nothing. I was so embarrassed and all I wanted to do was run, hide, and cry. My husband, in his defense, told my mom that she needed to leave his home and she had no right to be in his face. There I stood, still in shock, but trying to calm my husband down, as I could see him trying to self contain his anger all while my teen tried to calm my mother down. It was complete fuckery. My husband decided that this ignorance wasn't worth his time and husband decided to leave our house. Not to cool down and come back, but wouldn't come back until my mother was gone. Oh, and she was no longer welcomed based on her actions. What was I to do?

If the situation would have ended here, I would have calmed my mother down in efforts to understand what provoked her to bust into our bedroom. Outside of her being nosey, nothing was said or done to either one of us for her to think that we were in danger or our disagreement had become physical. I would have been able to calm my husband down and him know that no one (including me) has the right to make him leave his home. However, the situation didn't end there. My mother still fueled by rage had more to give. I was devastated, in tears, and working to figure out how I would resolve the situation. I called my husband in efforts to figure out where he left too and hopefully calm him down. My attempts failed, yet while I was trying to get my husband to return home my mother let off into a fueled rant of her own. "Let him go!" She kept repeating that I should let him walk away.

FRIENDS & FAMILY

Her reassurance was rooted in her own selfishness. She wanted me to be on "her side" and pull away from my husband based on her actions. "You, don't need him," she said, "we will help you." I responded with "Mom, that's my husband not my boyfriend." She responded with, "You don't chase no man." Agreed, but again this wasn't a random ass boyfriend, this was (is) my husband. To end her rant her last comment to me was, "I knew this would never work. I was just waiting for something like this to happen."

This is when I took a hard pause. Forget calling my husband. I lost all care in trying to console my child. I had to process the words that just came from my mothers mouth. Simply put - My mother had never seen hope for my marriage. A marriage that she showed excitement for. A man that she showed love to during his lowest times. To me all I saw was that my mom showed her truest of colors and had been silently awaiting my downfall.

The level of disrespect and fuckery and overall anger I felt was new to me. This hurt worse than any thing that occurred. It forced me to see my family in a new light. Not a light of positivity who supports my goals and dreams, but a dark, dim, light of despair. All I knew was that this cut deep and would take time if it was to ever repair itself. If it could be repaired. Not only because of what was said, but mostly because of who it came from - my mother of all people.

This situation showed me that even the person you regard to the highest degree, the person you might have the utmost respect for, can and will openly disrespect you with NO regard for your feelings. This situation made me understand that blood bonds do not heal wounds. Our familial ties do not place a heartfelt coating over the years of bullshit we force ourselves to put up with. Family ties are not a pass for any type of fuckery hurled your way. Period!

Your situation may not exist or may not exist in a similar fashion as mine. It may exist with a different person in your family or with a friend. Whomever it is, the title that they have in your life will NEVER give them a pass to step on you, shit on you, treat you as less, or blatantly disrespect you. Disrespect outside of your sight counts too. We all hate to believe hearsay, but half of the time it's true. If someone close to you is bold enough to say anything less than positive about you to others, then let the heavens open and give them the Godly courage to say it to your face. If not, then let this relationship stay right where it was going…nowhere.

NO, MY FAITH DOES NOT FORCE MY FORGIVENESS

Now this is my truth and you all can feel how you want to feel about this. Since many of us were raised in the church, we were all taught to Forgive and Forget, because that's what Jesus would do. Colossians 3:13…Forgive each other, as the Lord has forgiven you…. Well, thank the heavens I ain't Jesus and everyone is not a Christian. This one lesson has crippled so many of us into letting people treat us like garbage our whole lives. This one sentence allows for people to make you feel small, weak, insignificant, only for you to "turn the other cheek" and act like it never happened in search of an internal peace and holy afterlife that we assume has our name on it. One can only assume, but I'm sorry, I have too much life to live here in the physical form to continue to let others bully me into forgiveness.

You do not have to forgive and/or forget anyone wrongs against you on the basis of your religious beliefs. Repeat that two times again. Why? Because if you feel that someone has wronged you and you choose to remove them from your life, then that is a choice YOU get to make. No, they don't get the benefit of feeling better by receiving your forgiveness before they change their messed up actions permanently. No, your premature forgiveness allows them to walk around with no accountability for their behavior, most likely doing the same actions to someone else and probably you again too. **YOU DO NOT HAVE TO FORGIVE ANYONE. YOU DO NOT HAVE TO FORGET THEIR ACTIONS.**

This is family and friends included. Often times the people closest to us can do some of the worst things to us.

FRIENDS & FAMILY

Things that make us question the quality of our life. Behaviors that make you question what you did to deserve that treatment. Actions that cause trauma and depression. In most cases, there is no excuse for their actions and their behavior. Sometimes people are just fucked up or miserable and want to hurt others. Whether it be in a moment or that is just the way they are wired. Hurt people, hurt people. You do not deserve to be hurt in any way or by anyone. We must Say NO to rationalizing the behavior. Making excuses for the way others treat you without regard for your feelings.

We try to find a way to blame ourselves or justify the actions. This also forced me to Say NO to immediate forgiveness and forced memory loss (i.e., forgetting). Bitch, I don't have dementia and I am hopefully I'm a few years away from having Alzheimer's. I will not lie myself into believing that unfair treatment is ever acceptable. YOU deserve the ability to forgive in your own time, if ever. Forgiveness is not required and no your life does not end because you choose to withhold your forgiveness. Forgetfulness will not help you move on either, especially if the person (friend or family) has not truly changed their actions. Therein lies the problem.

We force ourselves to both forgive and forget the actions of someone towards us, but what is the requirement for the person who did us wrong?

FRIENDS & FAMILY

To get pass number 6,951 without changing their jacked up ways. Yeah, it's a No for me. Forgiveness is earned and for me its a tough one too earn, right up there with trust. This isn't applied to small actions - because usually an "I'm Sorry" or "I Apologize" suffices to resolve a minor issue. I'm talking about major mistakes. I will not even work to compile a list of what is major and what is not or which situations are easily forgivable and which ones aren't. If you have to question if your situations falls into this category then you might need to pause on your forgiveness, hold up on forgetting, and take a breath before dishing out that pass to that individual.

We also force religion to determine our decisions assuming its a one solution, fix all band-aid. In all honesty, it's not. Your God, Your Jesus is not the one being disrespected. (S)he is not the one who was embarrassed or made to feel less than by the actions of someone close to them. YOU experienced the pain, YOU dealt (or are dealing with the trauma). Your God does not have to deal with this person on a consistent basis moving forward. Forgiveness is not theirs to give, it's yours.

To own your forgiveness you first must **Free Yourself From Grudges**. Where we do go wrong is holding grudges. If you are losing sleep or have altered your life in a major way because of how someone treated you, then I advocate for you to find an outlet. Mine was therapy.

FRIENDS & FAMILY

It's available and it's a beautiful thing. Especially when the issues revolves around your family. Often times our issues with family are deep rooted, years in the making, and we do not come to an understanding that issues are still present until we are well into our adulthood. When we fight with ourselves about someone else's actions, we are giving them the power. You can Say NO to giving space and time in your life to anger. The individual who hurt you, whether friend or family, is not impacted by your grudge. You are. To remove this anger from your life, Forgive Yourself.

For what? For allowing yourself to alter how you live, how you think, or what you know about yourself based on the actions of your family or friends. Free yourself from a mental hold over whatever the situation is. Give the situation away. Give it to your God, the Universe, Your Therapist, A Good Friend, A Neutral party, whomever who will not judge you and make you feel that you owe anyone other than yourself something. Let go of the hold on your heart and be free to say sorry to yourself.

With self forgiveness comes honesty. We can be honest with ourselves to say that we overlooked and made excuses for those we loved. Those who we trusted the most. Those who we valued and who we thought valued us. You were not wrong, but you learned a lesson that will only help you moving forward.

Another honesty lesson learned is that many of us who lost a friend or a family member never tell them why we fell back, why we stopped talking. I know I've said, "They know why I don't fuck with them!". In reality they probably do not because they did not see the error in their ways. They never see their treatment of you as an issue.

Your truth rest in your ability to communicate. I'm not advocating for you to call or even physically see someone who has hurt you, caused pain, or trauma in your life. Not at all, but if you do not let it go, then you continue to allow the situation to have power over your life and take time away from yourself. You again give them the power over your ability to be at peace. The truth is that **They Do Not Have Power Over Your Happiness.** They never did and it only felt like they did because you gave it to them. So communicate with yourself. Write it down. Pen a letter. Type an email. Scream it or Cry it out. However you see fit, get it out, send it off, trash it, and Let it Go.

MY FEELINGS ARE VALID AND WILL BE ACKNOWLEDGED

Feelings and Pain go hand in hand with Forgiveness and Family and Friends. How many times have you told someone, whether family or friend, that what they did or said hurt your feelings? If you have someone of sound mind, they will acknowledge your hurt and pain and apologize. Normally no one intends to hurt you, but then there are the others. The ones who do not accept your truth. The ones who will fault your feelings on your inability to control your emotions. The creators of excuses and who try to rationalize their actions. The people who live to invalidate your feelings and/or pain because they are not ready to be accountable.

My Story: Thanksgiving Fuckery (Continued)

Through Thanksgiving, the situation did not immediately resolve itself. My mother felt she did no wrong and "just said what everyone else was thinking." That made it hurt even more. Damn, you were having conversations with others about my marriage and its impending dissolution behind my back and who was everyone else? I tried four times to get my mother to understand how her words hurt me to my core. How her words had created a wedge between her, my husband, and myself that would take time to heal. I told her she needed to apologize for her actions.

That is where I made my first mistake. My mother said she didn't need to apologize for anything. She then began to rally my other family (my dad and my sister) to "understand" her viewpoint and let them know how disrespectful my husband was to her. How he cursed at her and in her presence, but never informed them of her actions.

FRIENDS & FAMILY

Telling the person to apologize for their fuckery to make me feel better. Fuckery is their trade. It is what they are good at. We cannot force anyone to acknowledge their wrongs just as no one can force us to recognize the great in ourselves. We do it on our own time. In most situations the ones who have wronged us see no wrong in their ways. Your feelings are an after thought. Pain? Did they physically harm you? Were you injured? No. So where is the pain if they cannot physically see it and we do such an amazing job at masking it in their presence? It still exist, but we allow it to consume us and eat away at our well being because we don't know how to put a stop to their actions.

With my situation, now instead of dealing with one family member I had multiple people coming at me about what occurred. Not in support of my decision to correct my mother, but rather to persuade me to forgive my mother and look past her indiscretions. I could't believe it. My mother had emotionally manipulated the hell out of the situation and was now playing the victim. This is key when seeking to have family and friends acknowledge that their actions have caused pain. Your decision to continue life without them has now caused them pain. They will inform others of the pain that you have caused them without providing information about the backstory that led to the current situation. They may emotionally exploit the situation.

FRIENDS & FAMILY

Now they are the victim and you are the aggressor. You are now the problem and once again the cycle restarts itself.

Seeking Acknowledgement of your Feelings and Pain

Forced into Forgiveness Turned into the Aggressor

The cycle in which you seek to have your family and friends acknowledge your hurt. Understand the pain they have caused. Only to have it turned on you to where you are now the cause of their hurt. You are the aggressor and now are feeling forced to forgive to resolve the issue. It stops here. NO - Your pain and your feelings towards the original situation remain valid, whatever the situation may be. NO - You do not owe someone an explanation for why you hurt or feel the way you do. Your pain is your pain. You let them know they hurt you and that is all they deserve. They do not deserve the ability to direct your pain or to tell you how to feel. In the end, YOU will break the cycle. Family and friends who are unable to acknowledge the fact that their actions hurt you do not deserve a seat at YOUR table. When they are ready to acknowledge their actions and have a conversation in efforts to resolve the issue, then you determine where in your life they are invited back. Only YOU get to make that decision. Not them. Not others who have nothing to do with the situation.

YOU own this situation, YOU own your pain, and YOU own your healing, whatever it may look like.

My Story: Thanksgiving Fuckery (The End)

In a last ditch effort to hopefully make my mother understand the pain she caused, I tried to make her understand on our drive to the airport. I worked to explain to her my hurt. I tried to convince her that my husband and I were fine. Our marriage, which had never been marred by any scandal or infidelity, was just fine. I wanted her to own her actions and simply apologize so I could start to heal. To no surprise, she wouldn't budge.

No acknowledgement of her actions and her last physical words to me were, "If you don't like what I have to say, then don't fuck with me.", and my mother exited my vehicle to catch her flight. I balled my eyes out in the drop off zone of the airport. The only thing that stopped me from losing my shit at the airport was an officer who knocked on my window to force me to move my car.

In the end, we are only responsible for ourselves. We are responsible for owning our actions and for holding ourselves accountable for our errors. We are not responsible for forcing anyone to see the error in their ways. It is a fight that is hard to win, especially when someone is not ready to be accountable.

You know your pain is real. Your feelings are real and do not waste your time putting energy into changing others. Use that same energy to put time into your healing. That self focal time to acknowledge your hurt, find an outlet, and release the pain and entrapment over your life and time.

<u>NO, I AM NOT RESPONSIBLE FOR MY FAMILY OR FRIENDS.</u>

Look at you! Through everything you have been through you have accomplished something amazing. Life. You are living, when they thought they had stopped your life. You are rising to the occasion when they tried to slow up your progress. You are making YOU a priority when they tried to make you feel insignificant. These are all accomplishments that are not tied to tangible items. They are not tied to things, but what about when others tie themselves to the things you have accomplished? What about that one family member who is always getting bailed out by someone? Or that one friend who never has it but always "has it" because someone makes a way?

Maybe it's literally luck. There is some being or power that watches over these people to never ever let them truly hit rock bottom and always makes a way out of no way. NO. Usually it's someone, maybe you, who is making the way appear when it wasn't meant to be. Listen, you are not responsible for the well-being of your family or friends. If you are able to assist someone through a rough time in their life or have the means to invest in a friends dream, by all means do it! But if you find yourself making excuses for a sibling or friend and that excuse ends up taking away time and money from your life, you need to reassess and ask How Are You Really Helping?

If you are creating a way for others and not allowing them to learn or do the work themselves then you are an enabler. In the end this may cause resentment, especially if that person does not engage in the same type of charity when roles are reversed or you are in need. With our siblings, we never want to see anyone out on their ass, especially when kids are involved. Many of us have watched our parent(s) help when their wasn't any help to give. Our families have gone out on limbs and put themselves into debt or risky situations for people who repeat the same actions.

My Story: Thievery At Its Finest

In the late 90's I had an aunt that outwardly had it "going on" as we used to say. We will call her Aunt Maxine. Maxine drove luxury vehicles and her house was laid. The newest furniture and the latest everything. As a kid, I was jealous because it <u>looked</u> like she was rich. Her kids had all the toys and video games, she travelled and held parties that were talked about for days. My aunt was poppin'!

FRIENDS & FAMILY

One winter, my grandmother was hospitalized. During her stay in the hospital, my aunt Maxine didn't come to see her often, if ever. This struck most of the family as weird being that she was the baby of the family and had a deep connection with my grandmother. Nevertheless, my family overlooked it as the focus was for my grandmother to heal and get discharged. During the hospital stay, my mother visited Maxine and noticed that she had done some redecorating. New living room set. New appliances. The works. My mother took this to seem odd because who shops while their mother is in the hospital? My aunt stated that this was how she was "grieving" because she didn't know if my grandmother would make it.

Welp! Grandma made a full recovery and returned home to discover that she was a victim of identify fraud while in the hospital. Yes, someone had stolen my 70+ year old grandmothers information and opened accounts, racking up debt upwards to $5,000. But why? But who? Many loved and respected my grandmother so we were all at a lost on who would do such a horrible thing. **The who was my Aunt Maxine.**

She had used my grandmothers social security number to open up accounts to purchase new furniture and new appliances while she was in the hospital. Her own selfishness and desire to impress others overshadowed her love and care for her own mother. This was my first insight to how wrong family can do one another. The family was appalled and came down hard on my Aunt Maxine. She needed to pay my grandmother back and return the items to close the accounts, right? Not a chance.

FRIENDS & FAMILY

My grandmother had a soft spot for Maxine. She (my grandmother) had always been the "way maker" for her and Maxine knew no other way. You see Maxine had been known for being a "creative story teller" over the years and lying her way into adulthood. Whether it was lying to her siblings, lying about others throughout town, or lying her way out of near death situations, my grandmother always bailed her out. This time was to be no different. My grandmother forgave my Aunt Maxine and paid off the debt herself.

Maxine kept the furniture and moved on as if the situation never happened. My family was furious. How dare she take advantage of their mother like that. She was called everything except a child of God, except to her face. At family gatherings the issue was never spoken of and this is where I learned that you sweep it under the rug for the sake of peace. That what it looks like should overshadow what it really is. I learned that you can enable someone to their death (literally and figuratively).

The moral of my story is for you not to give your time and/or yourself to being that enabler. Be the truth in someone's life today to tell them what it really looks like from the outside looking in. Say NO to enabling the wrong in their life and enable them to get help and make change. Empower someone towards positivity. With our family and friends, being honest is hard. Who are you to tell them that their lifestyle, how they live, or their ways are unhealthy? You aren't a doctor, you aren't an expert, you are just you?

NO, if your time, energy, or money are contributing to their ways you are now a responsible party and have earned the right to Say NO to the Shit Show. As an enabler you are equally responsible for everyone they hurt with their actions. So take a stand today and no longer assume the responsibility for the pain others cause to themselves or others around you.

You are Not Responsible for Your Family or Friends, but you are responsible for protecting yourself from their bullshit. Be ready for the backlash. Be ready to possibly lose a loved one. If this happens, it is okay because change hurts and change often takes time to come to terms with. Once they understand where you stand and what you will (or won't) stand for, your relationship will forever be changed and YOUR life will improve.

<u>NO, MY ACCOMPLISHMENTS ARE NOT YOUR SHORTCOMINGS</u>

Many of our friends and family members handle our success through life with grace and positivity. They are proud of the jobs and titles you have held (or hold). They love to tell others how you made it and the adversity you overcome to make it. Success is sweet. So why does it not always feel this way with our friends and family. Do we have the wrong friends? Maybe some of our family members do not understand how hard you busted your ass to get where you are.

FRIENDS & FAMILY

The pain and trauma you experienced to get what you've accomplished. Why can't they just be happy for you?

This is yet another area that we will hold up space in our lives, downplay our happiness, so that we can make others feel better. For me it has played in out in a variety of situations with friends and family. It took me a while to root for myself as it was common for me to downplay my personal success. No, I am no millionaire (hopefully one day) and I haven't created the next best tech invention, but I am successful in my own right. Remember that success if relative. What success looks like for you WILL NOT look the same for someone else near and dear to you. Your path is just that, YOUR PATH. It was carved out for you and when it is your time and everything is aligned, nothing can stop you but you. So why do our friends and family still hate on our happiness at times?

They Want Control - not physically, but psychologically. You reaching the level of success that you have or achieving major goals was not in their sightline for you. People often categorize others they grow up with in the same box as them. We all have the same opportunities, went to the same schools, grew up in the same neighborhood, but **we are not the same**.

Your drive is different. Your dreams are rooted in what you saw for yourself, not what they saw for you. When their expectations don't match your reality it can force a resentment that you are not responsible for. Have you ever heard someone close to you say, "You don't need to do all of that" when you express interest in trying something new? I have and often. It is usually from those who haven't accomplished much or couldn't see that sort of success in themselves. Again, this is mental control.

At times, I allowed myself to succumb to their vision for my success. How crazy does that sound - I allowed for someone else's vision for my life to determine my success. Take control of your life and Say NO. NO to allowing someone to place their narrow vision over your life. NO to their ability to place their constraints on your growth. **Your potential is NOT limited by their complacency**. You Are Not Them. You are YOU and YOU ARE AMAZING.

Personal Insecurities - This is when people set a benchmark for you based on their own success. Many of us have family members who wouldn't know the first thing about starting or running a successful business, but we allow them to deter our dreams of working for ourselves. We have friends who haven't stepped outside of their comfort zone to learn something new ever! Now you're stuck too because Misery Loves YOUR Company. When you change the benchmark, they are thrown off. They don't know what to do and now their message to you is rooted in their personal fear. When you made the choice to find greatness you created distance and unfortunately the distance may increase and they fear you will leave them behind. Do Not Stop! You are the change they need. This is not for you to personally attack someone's accomplishments, big or small, but to encourage. Empower them to step out and trust themselves.

Encourage them to try something new and be willing to share information on how you accomplished your goals.

They are Mad at Themselves - For most people it isn't about you at all. It is about them. When family and friends are not willing to show you grace and positivity, it can be because you made sacrifices that they are not willing to make. Your determination and willingness to make a way only makes them resent the choices they made in their lives. Their frustration is rooted in feeling stuck in their current way of life. What you will not do is apologize for their way of life. Unless you are directly responsible for their way of life, their feelings of inadequacy have NOTHING TO DO WITH YOU. A key word here is sacrifice. Those who are successful said YES to themselves and gave up the bullshit. They did take away time from their friends, family, time wasting activities to say YES to their Success. When our friends and/or family are unable to make change, this is in no way your fault. Do not allow someone's anger towards themselves to attack your success, near or far.

You Broke the Rules - Some of us grew up in areas where the bar for success was low. Girls have babies and get on state assistance. Dudes get killed or go to jail. We all have friends and family who deal with these circumstances on a daily basis. For some of us, this may have been our situation that was the catalyst for change. When our friends and family consider us their equals (we are all in the same place and race together) things are good. When you suddenly "make it," now they question your how. Did you cheat? Who helped you out? Now you're constantly defending your hard earned success at every turn to prove what you had to give up to get what you deserved. The question to them is: What is your reason for following broken rules?

No one said you cannot have success, but the mind is a powerful construct. When we surround ourselves with individuals, blood or not, who cannot see success for themselves they may not be able to visualize it for you. You have the choice to remove these individuals from your immediate life to move towards your success. In the end, the only rules that apply are those you make for yourself.

I love my family. I love my friends. I am only responsible for me. I will continue to tell myself this as it is true, but interactions with people can make it difficult to let go of carrying their world on your back. We are our ancestors wildest dreams and if you could gift success to everyone, you would. We can't. You can gift yourself with the ability to let go and sometimes love from afar.

FRIENDS & FAMILY

Your peace comes above all else and family and friends can either be it or detract from it.

In short, all you can try to do is offer what time you have available to help others help themselves. Remember we can show others the way to make change, but you cannot be the change they need. You also should only be making a way for those who are worthy. Your assistance and advice are more valuable than any money because it is knowledge. **Summed up - Whether Friend or Family, You Deserve Respect and Love if they desire it in return.**

LOVE

"We accept the love we think we deserve."

Stephen Chbosky

LOVE

Love is a hard one to set boundaries and rules for. Why? Because often times it involves our heart more than our head. Most times, our head is never in the game to begin with. Ugh, the mistakes that love has led me into or better yet, the mistakes I made because I didn't look past love. I'm not talking about loving our family, our friends, or even a pet. Nope. I'm talking about the love we choose to give to strangers. The love we willingly lather others with in hopes of reciprocity. The love that we say will make us complete. The love we seek to find within lust. The love that breaks us down and makes us question our being. I'm talking about that kind of love. I am often able to Say NO to a lot of other things, with time and little guidance, but love has ALWAYS been an area of struggle for me.

I've told myself that I need to be single. I've said time and time again that I will not settle. I have refused to put up with the same bullshit. Only to let myself down because the heart is weak and so is my flesh. I also enjoy my flesh with someone else's flesh and that is where my head has gone out the window in the past. So how do we do better? By being honest with yourself first and foremost. Love is not the culprit, we are. We look past the lies and bullshit of the last person who broke your heart because you wanted it to be "different". You chose to take them back for the 50th time after being ghosted because this time would be different.

You put up with the disrespect because you have devoted some much energy and time into this relationship. You put your dreams on pause because you needed to help them make their dreams a reality. When you sum it up, we revert back to the beginning of this book. You, once again, put yourself on the back burner and put someone else ahead of you.

Your love comes with rules and boundaries. You are an amazing person who attracts all kinds of people into your life. We all know that whether they are in your life for a lifetime or a simple season, there is a lesson to be learned from the love that you will share. Where we often go wrong is putting the wrong rules and boundaries into place for the wrong people. Read that again. We often lose out on great love because we set rules for people and not ourselves. Why would you require one partner to respect you and treat you like a queen (or king) and then allow another to walk all over you like trash? What was the difference between the two? If the difference was materialistic or cosmetic, then you need to reassess your priorities. Someone's looks or what they can offer you NEVER grants them a pass to treat you like less than you deserve. So my first NO of love is:

<u>NO, ME BEING SINGLE DOES NOT PERMIT DISRESPECT</u>

Relationships can sometimes be treated like jobs. In the past, like a job, I felt like I needed to ensure had some security

LOVE

before moving on from one relationship. It is always easy to depart from something, anything, when you have something else waiting in the wings. Relationships are no different. Hopping from one love to another feels easier on the heart and your head. You feel that you don't have to dwell on what didn't go right. You have this new person to allow you to focus on the good with them. Why focus on healing with you feel like you are focused on happiness, right?

Wrong, but we will get into this in the next topic. But what happens when the time between lovers goes longer than expected. If this were a job, you'd be a little worried. Your savings (let's call it your love storage), might hold you over for a few months, you may feel like you are making time to get back to "you", but then the reality sets in. The holidays roll around and you realize it is just you. You now feel like you are in a drought, why haven't you found a decent prospect? What is going on? After the 3 - 6 Month period, maybe even 12 months or more, our good friend Loneliness may creep up onto your doorstep. You may also invite in other emotions like Depression, Anger, Sadness, Confusion, but in the end you come to the reality that you are with only yourself and this is okay.

Single parents may toss themselves into our kids. Work-a-holics toss themselves into work. Some of us set out on a Ho-Tation of sorts and start physically testing the sexual waters.

LOVE

However; many of us open ourselves up to trouble. The trouble of letting down our guard, lowering our standards, and accepting anything, specifically disrespect in efforts to say we have a relationship. Just because any of us are single for any amount of time does not permit anyone to come into your life and treat you like garbage. I have been in situations where I have accepted a man into my life to fill a void. It had been a year or more of being single and I wanted love. When choosing what I thought was love, I ended up choosing lust and stressing myself the hell out.

I ended letting someone tell me that I needed to accept their attitude, their mistreatment, their disrespectful tone and actions because "you couldn't find a man" before them. This was my cycle for years. No one wants to be the consistent "single friend". It wasn't fun to be alone during the holidays all of the time. And as I said, physical affection feels good. I now realize that no matter any length of time that you decided to free yourself from the bondage of a relationship, you do not deserve any type of mistreatment once you decide to re-enter the world of dating. Just because you have chosen to remain single does not mean you are LONELY! Many people are in relationships and VERY LONELY, remember that! The fact is that when you decide to jump back in and put your heart in the hands of another - THEY MUST RESPECT IT and TREAT IT LIKE GOLD. You are worth so much. You deserve everything you ask for and NEVER let anyone else tell you otherwise.

I WILL TAKE TIME TO TRANSITION, HEAL, & PREPARE FOR REAL LOVE.

While realizing that no matter how long I was single, that my heart and feelings deserved to be respected, I often didn't realize that my time to be single was often too short lived. A year may sound like a long time, but I've given much more time in my life to the wrong people who took so much more from me (mentally and physically). Many of us have had someone in our lives tell us that, "Men are like buses..." and "There are plenty of fish in the sea". Well, apparently I was waiting on the wrong route and no one ever gave me the map to get to this sea of people. I kept riding the same musty buses, figuratively and literally, and wading in the same shallow ass pool with everyone else. It was a continuous cycle that led nowhere.

I treated relationships like jobs. I desired love in my life so bad at one time, that I felt why leave any downtime to be alone. I was a good woman, I think I'm cute, and let's get it poppin'. So as one situationship ended, I was gassed up and ready for the next. What never occurred to me is that I deserved time to process, heal, and understand my past relationships.

LOVE

This time was required before I could fully give myself to the next person coming into my life. I wanted to prepare for the real love that I deserved. I also could never heal from my past because I kept acting like I wasn't hurt. What I had to first Say NO too was rushing. There was no reason why I needed to rush into any relationship.

This was my immaturity forcing me to make decisions without much thought. Using temporary feelings to make permanent decisions. What I got out of rushing was absolutely nothing but pain. Either someone caused pain to my heart or was a pain in my ass, but the biggest pain was to my being. Every person I gave myself too took a little piece of me with them. If I loved hard, they took a piece of my heart each time I put it out there for them to break. Every lie, every word of disrespect, every time they cheated, a piece of my heart broke. With the pain they gave me, I then transferred it to others, and others, and others. For the ones I disrespected, they received my mind. I lost a little more of me every time we argued, every time I chose to belittle them, every time I thought about being with someone else while giving my body to them. I wasn't doing myself any favors. I had to heal. You deserve to heal, but how do we heal?

This isn't about packing up someone's stuff and throwing it out of your place. That helps, but that's surface. Healing isn't complete by blocking someone out of your phone and social media. That's surface healing. Real healing takes place within you. Real healing means understanding your thought process in the choices that were made. It means forgiving yourself for stepping outside of your truth to make someone happy. It means giving yourself the space to get back to YOU.

The first requirement is to let go and accept what is real. Yes, you are really single and yes, the relationship wasn't worth your time. If you're hurt because you thought someone loved you, then live in the reality of that hurt. Don't force it away and don't cover the pain with another vice. Live in it, feel it, and take baby steps to move forward each day. NO, you aren't broken and NO, this won't kill you. You're learning to deal with the pain of change, not heartbreak, change is a skill that will benefit you.

Next, take some time to love on you. This goes back to Saying NO to Yourself. You have done that enough times and often times Saying NO to what is right is what leads us into horrible love situations. This time, Say NO to anything that takes you away from loving on YOU. Loving on you is a process of telling, showing, and proving to yourself that you are dope just the way you are. That a person supplementing your life does not change the fact that you are amazing. Date yourself. Take the time to figure out what you really enjoy and what irks you. Take the time to invest in you.

LOVE

You have the time that was put into that other person available now, use it to your benefit. Show you how amazing YOU can be and are in real life.

Reconnect with yourself spiritually. Meditation works for some, Prayer for others. Whatever your beliefs or choices, take some time to find solace and hear you. No, you aren't crazy for talking to yourself, you're sane for giving yourself space to be with your thoughts. Clear your head of any negativity that remains from any past relationship. The thoughts of inadequacy, the feelings that you weren't enough, the belief that you didn't deserve real love. Then reconnect with yourself physically. This may look different for all of us. You are still a living, breathing, beautiful person, who deserves a physical connection. Until you connect with yourself how will know that someone else has done it right? Take the time to LOVE on you and be the best version of you for whomever you CHOOSE to let into your life.

MY WANTS AND MY DESIRES ARE NOT UNREASONABLE

As you clear your head, mind, body, and soul of the garbage left behind from the undeserving, you now free yourself up to make space for those who deserve someone like you. Do you know what those people look like?

LOVE

Do you know what things you want from them and what you are willing to provide? Do you have a Love List? You do and it's probably in your head and contains physical attributes that your ideal partner must have in order to qualify for your time. Right? Funny, we all have one as I have had one since I was about 16. I used to have a spiral notebook to list out about 50 things that a man MUST have in order to become my husband (because marriage was a priority at 16, Ha!).

As I got older and referred back to this "list," I realized that the list would get shorter and shorter as time passed. I realized that I began to adjust my wants and desires based on those who were available to me. I realized that I was settling for whatever and making adjustments to what I truly desired. I again put ME on the back burner.

My rationale was that the guys I met had so many of the qualifiers (usually less than 10% of what I wanted) so that made it okay, we could build and work on the others. This is where the problem existed. I convinced myself that I did not deserve to have a choice in who wanted me. I made a list only to tell myself that this person, whom I created in list form, wouldn't want me. I wasn't "List Man"'s type. Now "List Man" was tall, dark, and handsome. Great job, good credit, and financially stable. Healthy, charming, and loving. He was a Unicorn in a field of trolls. Well , troll no more! **Your wants and desires are not unreasonable.**

LOVE

You have the right to remain steadfast in what you desire in a partner and what you expect to receive in return for your love. Simple as that! Anyone who tells you different is forcing you to settle for their standards. NO, Your Standards are not Their Standards. When you settle, you do a disservice to only yourself. You force yourself to conform to the wants and needs of others only to remain unhappy, still seeking the person you truly desire. Be true to you and go after what you want.

Now having a certain amount of qualifiers should be expected for anyone, but the more constraints you put on your "type" the smaller the pool. It is a fact. There are only so many unicorns made to your liking out here in the world - chances are your unicorn looks similar to someone else's unicorn tool. Do you settle? NO. Settling is for suckers, but you may have to compromise.

How you do define compromise versus settling? When we settle, we accept anything given to us. You wanted someone with a degree, you took someone who didn't and isn't remotely interested in furthering their education. You settled. Compromising is meeting someone who is currently in school, working towards completing their degree. They don't match your qualifier now, but will soon. It is okay to make compromises when finding the love you deserve. How many times and where you choose to compromise is up to you.

LOVE

What I had to learn is that there is a difference. Some things are not up for compromise. If you said you want someone that does not cheat and chose a person who has cheated in their past, that will NEVER qualify. NO, We won't compromise. Why? Because they changed? Unlikely. Are you gong to be the catalyst for their change or want them to show you they've changed? How? Or will you be worried that their old habits will resurface and always questioning if you made the right decision. In the end, Don't settle and go for what you deserve.

You want someone with straight teeth. You meet someone with a crooked tooth here and there. This is where we compromise because thanks to modern science and about $70 bucks a month, straight teeth can become a reality. I repeat, stick to your guns and go after what you WANT and what you DESIRE. Make your list and check it twice, and go for your ideal love.

MY PAST LUST WILL NOT DETERMINE MY FUTURE LOVE

For me this one was short and simple. Just because I make some messed up choices in love in my past, they WILL NOT determine who I date in the future. We all grow in various areas and our choice of love should be one of them. If you realized that the pool in which you are swimming is shallow and only resulting in heartbreak, then pack up and go swimming elsewhere.

LOVE

I do not care what town or city you live in, there are other places to hang and mingle and meet people besides where you are going now. NO, you won't make excuses for dating people who constantly shit on you. NO, you will no longer settle for someone who slept with someone you know personally. Stop that mess TODAY! Go after what is for you and expand your horizons.

If you want to try online dating, then give it 100% and try online dating. If it doesn't result in a long-term, everlasting love affair, then if nothing else you met some new people. At least you tried something new. If you have someone that you know that you've been interested in for a while (and they are single), show them some old-fashioned interest. Stop living in fear of life and in fear of finding real love. Putting yourself out there, especially in a new space and in a new way can be scary, but what is more scary is dating the same type of people that have left you hurt in the past.

What is most scary is that we often NEVER address why we make the choices in love that we do. Whether it be parental issues, past abuse, or living outside of our truth, your job is to be honest with yourself. Stop letting your past mistakes dictate the now. Get the help that you DESERVE and make a change in the way you operate in love. No one coming into your life deserves to deal with the baggage and brokenness that someone gave to you before them. It is not their fault. It is not their responsibility.

They are not responsible for healing you or unpacking it. Period. As long as we keep rehashing old fights with new partners and dragging old baggage into new ventures, your past lust (not love) will determine what type of relationship you fall into. The simple fix is to change YOU, your surroundings, to change the end result.

I love the saying, "Eagles Do Not Fly with Chickens". This means that everyone is not meant to be around everybody. Where do you classify yourself? Don't say Eagle and you're doing Chicken Shit! If you want to soar, in both love and life, the message is to change your surroundings and explore new opportunities in love. Doing the same things and expecting new results is pure insanity. Change for the goal you want to achieve.

THEIR RELATIONSHIP IS NOT MY RELATIONSHIP

Another area I had to tell myself Nah, was my bad habit of comparing what I had (or didn't have) to others. Correction, Other Women. I would see happiness among friends and familiar faces, I would question what they did, were doing, or were sacrificing to make sure their relationship looked happy. How did they make it last and mine didn't? I would come up with irrational assumptions, usually shitting on someone in my head, to justify why I was in the position I was with love.

LOVE

The easiest way to fail in love is to compare what you have (or want) to others or what you had in the past. Why? Because it is toxic. Every relationship is different and for good reason. What is good for one person may not be good for you. Another reason that comparison is toxic is because you are making an assumption off of a sliver of information. Yep, I'm talking about Social Media.

Social Media does not validate a relationship. Social media only allows you to see the bits and pieces, usually the happier times, that people want you to see. You don't get the full details, you get the kissy faces, the happy photos, and joyful memories reminding you of how long they've been blissful. You don't see the disagreements, the arguments, the disappointments, and the truth into the heartbreak (if it exist).

Do not feel bad as it's natural to compare as we do it in every part of our life. I do it now with our marriage. We will see a beautiful couple and I'll say, "We need to be more like that"... what I need to say is, "we need to improve on X area in our lives so that we can have Y". My relationship is not theirs and will never be. I have the partner meant for me who loves me and all that I bring to our union. I have someone who makes me excited to love them back and cheer them on through the good and bad. I have someone who I determined is worth going through the rough patches and disagreements with because our happiness is everything. I have MY relationship.

LOVE

You deserve your own relationship. Where the issues exist with comparisons are when you allow them to impact your relationship or how you date. You set an unreal expectation for yourself based on what someone told or showed you. Comparisons force us to, once again, lie to ourselves about what we really want. Now you're focused on what you think you need, because someone else has it.

If you're comparing a current relationship or situationship to someone you dealt with in your past, be prepared to be let down. It will NEVER be the same because they aren't the same. The walls and guards you protect yourself with only hurt you. The new person didn't break your spirit and until you heal, you are pushing someone to cause hurt in your life because you are projecting. Your projection of what you think will happen based on the past may speak it into existence. The hope that your new interest will treat you as good as your past love isn't going to happen either. They will treat you based on the boundaries you set in place. Why? **Because they aren't the other person**. You again set yourself up for failure if you're waiting for someone to meet the expectation of the past. It isn't fair. It wouldn't be fair if they asked the same of you. Just stop doing it.

A suggestion for happiness is to seek to understand. What is it about someone's relationship that you like? If they are in your circle, be willing to step out and ask questions.

See if they're willing to share the truth (good and bad) with you. Not to be salacious, but rather help you create a guide for the type of love you desire. As a married woman I am always willing to speak the truth about my situation. I believe that sharing is caring. Not to tell all of our business, but to help others develop a road map for the love they seek.

Seek to understand your past as well. What about your past relationships caused you to put up a guard. Have you reflected on the areas that you need to heal? What about your past relationship was wonderful? Is it reasonable to expect the same treatment from someone new or was the treatment truly based on that specific person? These are real questions because again, every unicorn is not the same. Your love is YOUR LOVE and if you let go of what was, and focus on what is to come, you can make it some of the best love you've had (or will have).

<u>NO, I DON'T NEED LOVE, I DESERVE REAL LOVE</u>

It is a very common misconception that as women, we NEED a relationship to be complete. That we NEED someone to keep us warm at night. That after a certain age, we will be ALONE forever if we aren't tied down. Social media has perpetuated this lie, comedians make jokes about single women, and we've all seen our friends conversation change when they

LOVE

find new love. Ha! Lies, they are all lies. I too am even guilty of thinking that a relationship was a need.

Truth is that you don't NEED anyone to love you, but you DESERVE real love. What this means is that you do not need to root your joy in another person. Doing so will leave you wide open for hurt and pain. A beautiful and happy relationship can be a source of joy, but you DO NOT need a relationship to be happy.

The goal is for you to find your personal happy. Once you meet someone they are a bonus, and should add to your happiness. You are a WHOLE person, with WHOLE ass goals, and WHOLE feelings. You are WHOLE. No man (or woman) is going to make you complete. If this is your thought process, then you have so much more work to do. If you felt broken when someone left you or broke up with you, you have work to do. That work is finding what makes you complete within you.

Someone else's love for you is not guaranteed. People are living, changing beings, that change their mind all of the time. If you find someone who is willing to make you a priority in their life and give you the love that you deserve, then let them add to you. What we let people do is feel as though they make us who we are. That they complete us as a person. Then when they let us down, we lose ourselves. **You are complete with or without them.** You just need to understand what a complete you looks like. When are you Complete You...

LOVE

You Celebrate YOU: Life's little moments are exciting with others, but it is an amazing feeling when you can celebrate yourself. Instead of waiting for others to celebrate small victories in your life and validate your dopeness, you must celebrate yourself. No one, and I mean no one, is going to celebrate you like you! You know the hard work and struggles you had to push through, you know what you sacrificed and put off to get what you have, you know how much you had to change to reach these new heights. No one can take away what you worked hard for. A partner in your life will be proud of you, but until you are proud of yourself if won't mean a thing. Take yourself out to dinner. Buy yourself a new outfit or trinket. Make a post about yourself and your accomplishment. Those who really love you will provide more support than you can handle. We don't worry about the others.

You Believe in Yourself: There have been so many times in my life that I let self doubt talk me out of going for what I want. I waited for someone to give me permission to go after my goals. I wanted for someone to step out on faith with me because I was too scared to go alone. This occurred for years on and off. In relationships, I wanted my partner to champion my goals like they were his. I wanted my hand held every step of the way, just in case I failed. I wanted someone to want my success in the same way I wanted it. I again, wasted time and lost out on opportunities because I didn't believe in ME.

When we are complete, our goals don't need to wait for anyone to validate them. Our goals are our goals and we know that we are capable of achieving them alone. If you are able to find a partner who encourages your success and helps you make a way, it still doesn't make your dreams theirs. You still need to believe in YOU. So many people wait for validation from the ones they love, only to find themselves waiting for the rest of their lives. If I would have waited for my husband to tell me to go back to school, I would have never gone. It is not his place to force me into anything. Your loved ones can suggest and recommend, but no one can force YOU to make change except for YOU. I have heard many people state that they left past loves because "they didn't support my dreams or help me with my goals". A better question is "how do you support your dreams and help yourself with your goals?" and "why are you waiting for anyone to have your back to move forward?"

Because you rooted your worth in this other person. You thought that you completing certain goals would make them happy for you. You again saw them as making you complete. Belief in yourself is knowing that you have the kit for making your goals a reality. You may pick up additional tools and skills along the way, but you are the way maker.

LOVE

Again, be complete in YOU and know that YOU ARE ENOUGH. A partner can add to your goals and help you further your dreams, but if you don't start alone then you will always be making others dreams your reality. But how do you know you're complete or making your way towards being complete within yourself?

Who You Love is Based on Your Worth: In the end, love is still a beautiful thing and you deserve to have it in its realest form. The love that you desire should be rooted in the fact that someone values every piece of you. That your future partner protects you like the gem you are. Take some time to develop your love list to understand what you want and deserve. You should include positive minded messages like:

They WILL accept me for who I am

I can be my TRUE self when I am with them

They will support and encourage me while I fulfill MY dreams

They believe that we can grow together and individually

They know that we can share everything: emotions and thoughts

We can speak to each other honestly without judgement

Communication is important to both of us for our relationship

Our challenges and difficulties will be an opportunity for growth

We are both happy individually and happier together

LOVE

Now this is just a start, but this list speaks to a woman satisfied with herself. The addition of a partner is an added benefit. When you know your worth, you will not have to search for the love you deserve. You will be so consumed with your dreams and making your goals a reality that the love will come to you. There is no desperation when you know yourself. Your confidence will no longer let you crawl into the arms of the wrong one. It is your personal responsibility to take care of yourself. Make a promise to yourself that you always remain Honest and True to yourself about your needs, desires, and wants in terms of love. You will ensure that joy and fulfillment exist in your life with or without a partner. **That no one but YOU can make you feel WHOLE.**

NOW WHAT?

"Whatever you decided to do, make sure it makes you happy"

Paulo Coelho

<u>BABY STEPS BOO</u>

For me, acknowledgement of the need to change was the biggest change I had ever made in my personal life. Yes, I had changed careers. I had even moved across the country with my family. I got married. I had a kid. Those all were changes that involved others . This change involved me and only me. I needed to say no and release myself from a lot of things. I am a "cold-turkey" type of person. I just want to start it and get to the finish line as quickly as possible. For many tasks in my life, this is done with reasonable ease and I can move on to the next. The personal change of removing myself and saying no wasn't a quick change. Hell, I didn't even know where to begin. Should I start with a person? Should I start with a thing? NO, I needed to start with me and the journey to the finish line didn't exist.

Deciding that you want to change is figuratively starting over. You have lived your life doing many things the way you were taught. The way we saw our family or parents do them. The way we always thought were right. To break a life-long habit is difficult. You may know no other way of life but the way you think you were designed. Now it's your turn to reshape the way you think, do, act, behave, and treat yourself. You get to   start fresh and set the rules and boundaries for how your life will move. This is not a race, there is no finish line, as your change will become constant.

NOW WHAT?

What you are preparing to change today, may not be relevant a week from now. The person you Say NO to today may no longer be a factor next month. The individual you are today will for sure NOT be the same person you see a year from now, if you want to change.

To begin the process for your personal change, you MUST take baby steps. We are all running too fast, every day, towards everything. We want everything to happen NOW. Our happiness, our success, changes in our health, and finding love. We approach change in the same way, always wanting it to happen immediately. This change is no different from anything else, it will take time. It will take you devoting time, on a daily basis, to see the change in your life so that you can live the life you desire. This change is to ensure you are no longer held hostage by someone else's wants on your life, but rather know the destiny you've planned for yourself.

In your quest for change, you will recognize your mini-victories. They will be small, realistic, quickly achievable, but no less an accomplishment towards the bigger objective - Reclaiming YOU!

MAKE A PLAN FOR THE PLAN

Now that you know you need to make change, you need to plan for taking action. Your plan will look similar to a check list, of sorts, but be more specific for the action you need to take to get back to YOU. You will need to be mindful of how your time is spent, who your time is spent with, and ensuring specific areas of your life are getting the time they deserve. When building out your plan, it must be mindful of the most important thing for this change to become a reality, YOU!

Write it Down

The most successful people in the world write things down. This isn't a myth, this is fact. The reason why is because it makes it real. It makes whatever is floating in your head, whatever empty words you say, into something tangible. You can see it, develop the plan behind the words, and put that plan into action. So your first step is to write it down.

You do not have to use some fancy journal or expensive notebook. You can use a simple spiral notebook or basic notepad, but you NEED something to capture your thoughts. You need a Capture Tool. Thoughts (and doubts) will hit you at every turn of your process to change. You need to capture them to be able to process why you felt that way? What were you doing when that thought came to you? Is this a thought you want to put action behind? Whatever it is, you need to get it out of your head. Writing it out will also allow you to watch your transformation occur on paper. In the beginning of change, doubt can overcome us.

NOW WHAT?

You won't believe that you can stick to change, you will assume that something will throw you off track, you will work to talk yourself out of the progress you are making. As time goes by, time becomes your friend. The time you devote to yourself will allow you to dig deeper into who you are. Time to do the work to know you, time to root yourself in your rules and boundaries, time to find clarity in your new process. Your thoughts will become less doubtful and more proactive. You will then look to put action to your words to make your change real.

Your Goals - All of them, no matter how far fetched you think they are - should be written down. You want to lose some weight - Write it Down. You Need to Address Your Sister's Disrespect - Write it Down. You Want to Go Back to School - Write it Down. You Want to Start an Online Business - Write. It. Down. All of it. Nothing is too big or too small for your list. If you don't write it down, this is you telling yourself NO again. You are saying, NO, that was stupid. NO, I can't accomplish that. NO, I'm not worthy. You are worthy and capable of accomplishing EVERY thing that comes to mind. Yes, it takes work but your ONLY competition in this life is YOU. If you say NO to you then you can NEVER expect anyone else to say YES to your dreams.

Break it Down: Your goals and changes are like a 3 course meal. You can't ingest them all at the same time. You will have to pick

NOW WHAT?

like 2 or 3 things to work on at one time as you are only one person and there are only 24 hours in any given day. The first step is to break your list down into manageable pieces. Pick the 3 things on your list that draw emotion. Yes, I want you to pick the 3 things that tug at your heart the most. I mean when you look at these things on paper, you might get angry, you might tear up, you might get turned up, but whatever they are they cause a reaction. This reaction is the energy that will propel you to complete them. You might have gotten this reaction when you were writing them down. **Keep that Same Energy as we break down how you will move through your list.**

Two years ago, my Top 3 Were

Address the Disrespect from my Family

Make Me a Priority

Go to Grad School

All of them were super vague, but all of them focused on ME. They focused on me saying NO to other people's priorities in my life and making me a priority for myself. In order to truly make any gains in accomplishing my goals, I had to beak it down into pieces. For Goal #1, I had to narrow it down.

NOW WHAT?

At some point and some time in my life, someone in my family had said something that could be construed as disrespectful. I wasn't talking about every little smart-ass thing anyone had said, but those who felt that disrespect was an acceptable norm with me. I needed to address those individuals, but how? This is what I needed to breakdown. I needed to address them in person and tell them how their actions made me feel. Not over the phone and definitely not in writing, I needed to do this in person.

They needed to hear the tone of my voice and see the emotion in my face. I didn't plan on playing a victim, but it is often a natural reaction for emotion to reflect our release of pain. The pain that I had suppressed for many years by telling myself, "No, it's not worth it to say anything" or "No, they don't care how you feel". Well, NO, they don't get to dictate what I hold onto or how I feel in their presence. They also deserved to know how their presence impacted others. This exchange was not to show them the power I had allowed them to have over me, it was to take my power back.

Taking your goals or areas of focus and breaking them down will help it become a little more real. It helps you understand the root of the issue. When you leave your Top 3 as they are, they can often be vague, hard to see where you need to start, and easy to throw away. The break down allows you to refine what you need to do and address the Who, What, When, Why, and How. You need to address all of these buckets to get to your action plan. My plan was:

What: Discuss the constant disrespect of me & lack of support of my goals

Who: Immediate Family

Why: I feel personally attacked and there is no justification for the disrespect.

How: In Person - Face to Face

When: ??????

Where I struggled was setting a when. I needed to solidify my plan and the action I wanted to take by putting a date to it. How important is something if you don't make time to make action?

Set A Date: It doesn't really become real until you schedule it. I mean set a time and place to make it really happen. This is with EVERY action you need to take in your life. You need to start improving your health, schedule the time in your calendar. You need to meditate, schedule the time in your calendar. You need to make time to work on your goals, schedule it. It seems easy when we talk about it. We sound like we have it going on when we discuss the how, what, and why with friends and family. The truth is in who is really making it happen by making the time.

NOW WHAT?

Look over your current schedule and think about all of the time wasters you fill your time with. The top time waster is our phones. It's a time waster because we often use it, not as a method to improve our lives (which it can and is designed to be), but rather as an escape. We use our phones to track the progress of everyone else's life and what they are doing with their time that we often fail to see the time we lost doing so. The time we GIVE to others is NOT making you money, it's NOT making your life better, rather it TAKES away precious time that you deserve to make change.

For me, making time to speak to my family wasn't at my choosing per se. I can't force someone to fly into my city for what might be a short conversation, NO, I have to make it happen when time presents itself. Are conversations best had when one party is unprepared? I'd like to say YES. The reason is that when you give someone time to prepare how they will respond to your truth, you give them time to craft their response. You want their truth, I wanted my families truth. Will it be pretty, most likely not, but you will at least understand where that person stands and how they feel about your truth.

The key is to stay ready and be prepared for the opportunity when time is available. For anything. Remember to remind yourself that the steps towards accomplishing any goals will not feel perfect on any try.

NOW WHAT?

The key is to try because if you don't even try to make time to accomplish your goals then they will forever live as dreams. Your time will then just be used to accomplish someone else's dreams. So, Make Your Plan (Write it Out) and Make Time to Execute Your Plan.

What Does Action Really Look Like?: Without action, NOTHING Happens. If you have decided to make yourself a priority, then that is the first action in making change. Small win! Congratulate yourself for that if nothing else, but there is more to be done. I watched for years as others made progress in their lives. Accomplished degrees. Wrote Books. Purchased Homes. Started Businesses. Started Families. Lost Weight. So many people around me were making all of these amazing things happen, but I felt stuck. My life wasn't moving at the same pace, my dreams weren't converting to a reality in the same manner, what was different about me from them. Why were they winning? Was it luck? NOPE! It was ACTION. The difference in many (not all) of the Have's and the Have Not's is simply ACTION. The Have's took action on a plan for their dreams that provided results. Your purpose is to say NO to any lack of action in your life. Your inability to stand firm on what you want, what you desire, and what you deserve. Saying NO to taking action for everyone else except for you. **Choose YOU and Take Action Today.**

NOW WHAT?

Back to my conversation with my family:

I had to take action. I chose a family holiday (this was years prior to the Thanksgiving Fuckery story, LOL!) and addressed my mother and sister in an upstairs bedroom in my home. Let me be the first to tell you, taking action IS NOT EASY! Especially when it's dealing with something you have been suppressing or putting off for years. I was scared as hell, but realized that my piece of mind moving forward was worth so much more.

Yes, the conversation was difficult. Yes, I cried and voices were raised. For me it didn't feel as though the issue was resolved because I cannot force people to understand nor accept my truth, but what mattered is that I stood in my truth. I accomplished a personal goal of addressing how I was treated and what I would no longer accept moving forward. I crossed it off my list and we moved on. We now move differently, but we moved on.

Action is designed for you to move differently, not for you to stay the same. If you look at your Top 3 and they've been your Top 3 for a while, then your current action plan isn't making sense. Start over and rewrite it, this time with purpose and intent. Be purposeful about why you chose your Top 3, how will they improve your personal life and keep you as the priority? Understand your personal intent as to why these Top 3 matter.

NOW WHAT?

Are they goals based on where you were in your life 10 years ago? Are they relevant to the person you are today? These are questions you need to answer and if the answer is NO, then reevaluate and determine a new plan of action.

Action also looks like honesty. When focusing on yourself and getting your life where you need it to be, it's okay to FAIL! You just need to fail fast and move on. I've been there and done it, hell we all have. Failed Relationship - Yep, done that! Failed Career - Been there too! Failed Myself - Yes, I've done this more times than I can count and allowed myself to get stuck here. I had to force myself to take action to move on past my failure. Focusing on the renewed goals and action plan to make the life I desire and deserve a priority.

Checking In and Check Ups: But how do you know if your action is even working? You won't unless you check in. Think of it like cooking a cake, you check on it periodically to make sure it's rising and it's baking correctly. You will have to do the same with your Goals, Deadlines, and Plan of Action - Self Assess. If you're using a capture tool of some sort and writing things down, your Self-Check In is a breeze. Schedule some time with YOU on a consistent basis (once a week is good start) to check in with yourself. I know it sounds crazy, but once again, you check in on EVERYONE else and EVERYTHING else, but think it's crazy to visit

NOW WHAT?

with you. NOPE! You deserve to check up on you. To determine where you are allowing yourself to get off track before you get too far gone. To see where you might need to reach out for help before you get too deep. To understand your feelings and what (or who) might be troubling you, thus blocking you from taking action. Your check in can be literally anywhere, but it should just be YOU. No, you aren't wrong for making time for you, you deserve time for you. You deserve time to understand how you can keep your action plan in tact. I do mine on Friday's and usually at work - a combined professional/personal check in.

I schedule the time as a Meeting with Myself. One hour is enough for me to review where I am with making the best life for myself. Making sure I've scheduled all of the time I need for me before giving myself to others. Not determining where I fit in with myself, but determining what time I will allow others to have. Some questions I ask myself when checking in are:

1. What made me the happiest this week?
2. What is one thing that I am most proud of this week?
3. What is one thing that I dropped the ball on?
4. How did I make time for me this week and why?
5. What hurt me the most this week and why?
6. How will I ensure that next week WILL be better than this week?

NOW WHAT?

My questions are geared towards action. The questions guide me to ensure I use the time to recognize what had the greatest impact on me personally. With a goal of reducing their future impact moving forward. Why should I allow the same issues to cause me grief? We need a resolution and I give my time to craft solutions, not cry over problems. This is no guarantee that new things won't impact how I feel, but I can take steps to adjust their impact on my life. This includes people too. In your action plan, for your goals, make time to assess where you are on a consistent basis. The biggest takeaway of your self assessment is watching your personal growth. One of the best feelings is looking back at something you wrote down in the past and being like, "I crushed that goal" or "I've come so far". To get to the finish line, you first have to make a starting point in order to witness how far you can go.

CREATING YOUR CIRCLE OF PURPOSE

Saying NO to everything and everyone else, doesn't mean that you subscribe to a life of being alone. Remember that the intent of saying NO is to solidify where you stand in how you allow yourself to be treated in various situations. It is intended to set the tone for how you maneuver in your life so no else can control your actions. For me, action is best propelled through motivation.

NOW WHAT?

I'm not talking about being motivated from watching people online, NO. I'm speaking about seeing real people, in real life, put in the work and operate as a resource for you when needed. **This is your circle of purpose**. Your circle of purpose is made up of people around you, not necessarily family, who encourage and support your change and growth in life.

These are not Yes-Men, these are people who you trust to be honest with you. These individuals make sure that they have clarity and focus on their goals, but are available to make time to help you find your clarity. The reason a circle of purpose is a necessity is because we cannot go it alone. If you believe that your way is the only way, that is narcissism. If you know that you can self assert yourself in situations and remain open to neutral feedback for improvement, then that is growth. You want a circle that breeds growth in your life. If you look around at who you consider to be in your circle, do you feel like they are encouraging your growth?

I am not talking about those who tell you to do the expected (ex: work). You don't congratulate a fish for swimming is what my elders used to say - basically someone shouldn't provide celebration for you doing the expected minimum. This is not someone helping you confirm your doubt when you're scared to try new things. No, those individuals have no purpose in your life.

NOW WHAT?

You want people who can see what you don't often times see within yourself. The people who read between the lines, hear your hurt, see your talents, and encourage you to make change to address these areas in your life. The individuals you encounter who leave you with a positive energy. Ask these individuals to be a part of your Circle of Purpose.

And what if you look at those close to you and can no longer see their purpose in your life? That is OK. We have all heard that people come into our lives for a Reason and a Season. Both are 100% true. If you determine that the people you are making time for are not sowing back into your life where it is TODAY, then again you are Saying NO to you. You are saying that you don't deserve to be around positive people who see prosperity in your life. I'm not talking about money, I'm talking about a two way exchange between parties who equally care about you being successful in your life. Not the people who only want the juicy details about our love life and to know if you've seen someone from 10 years ago because they've fallen off. These individuals are not worth your time.

You should be choosing people who have set personal goals and are taking action in their own life. Why? Because they become motivation for the action you need to take. You should choose others who are out of your age range (both older and younger). Why? They give you perspective into life.

NOW WHAT?

Those older than us have lived and can be a source of understanding of either what to do or what to avoid. Those younger are a source of life. You have the ability to speak positivity and honesty into someone's life at an age where guidance may not have been an option for yourself. Remember it's a collaborative process in your circle. You need to network with business owners, if you see this in your future. Learn from them, ask questions, give feedback, and help them grow so you can help yourself. You want to lose weight? Find others who are like minded in helping you stick to your goals. Not people to judge you or condemn your decision to have multiple cheat days. NOPE. People who are proud of your decision to make a change and seek to offer you genuine support to accomplish your goals.

The hardest part of your circle is that it will often times not look like your original circle of friends. Remember that time is a not a determinant on someone's place in your life. Just because I've known you for 20 years does not mean you add to my life today. Can we still be cool? For sure! Will you have a front seat to every dream, goal, plan of action, probably not and that is my choice. The reason is that I cannot continue to surround myself with the same individuals, some who may not yet see their purpose, and expect them to support me through my growth. I do not have to automatically cut anyone off because I decide to

NOW WHAT?

make change, but I will watch and understand who is for me and who isn't.

In the end, the goal is for all of us to do better no matter the stage we are in our personal lives. Once you accomplish one goal, you should ALWAYS be striving to accomplish the next one and so on. You should never be stagnant or complacent in your current position. This isn't a competition with anyone, but even maintaining your level of now takes work.

So when choosing to recognize the importance of your life, your ability to control your goals and dreams, you know that you can Say No Now and choose to say YES to YOU!

ABOUT THE AUTHOR

Nichele Nicole is an author with a passion for progress. Born and raised in Seattle, WA, Nichele stepped out on faith with her family and relocated to Houston TX for a fresh start. After making so many others a priority in her life and career, she realized that she no longer desired to be on the back burner. That included putting a focus on educational, career, and personal goals that would focus on her happiness. But what about others who were dealing with the same dilemma? Who would tell them it was okay to say, "I am a priority to me?" With that in mind, Nichele decided to write a personal story to others struggling to choose themselves. "I struggled to ask for others to help me find me. I don't want anyone else to struggle to find themselves and want to be a resource for all."

Say No Now is a book written to her new self from her old self. It is written to tell the past all of things you should say no too from what I've learned up to now. To improve the ability to assert yourself in some of the hardest areas of our lives - Ourselves, Our Family, Our Friends, and Our Love Lives.

Her focus on her happiness allowed for Nichele to successfully rise within her career in education, complete two degrees (MS and MBA in Business) and make time to continually focus on remaining the best version of herself.